Linda's Life and Lines

Excerpts from *Die Botschaft* letters
written by Linda Byler, 1991-1997

Laugh and learn with a talented storytelling mother relating her family's fun and foibles

Letters reprinted by permission of Die Botschaft, *Millersburg, PA.*

ISBN-13: 978-0-9795373-0-1

ISBN-10: 0-9795373-0-4

For additional copies contact:

WILLOW PRESS

15604 Paxton Road, Newburg, PA 17240

717-423-6045

printed by:

Carlisle Printing

OF WALNUT CREEK Ltd.

2673 TR 421

Sugarcreek, OH 44681

Dedication

First of all, I would like to give special thanks to David Blank and Old Mommy Byler (Lydia F.) for letting me use their *Botschafts.*

This book started as a scrapbook, saving memories for myself. I spent hours looking though *Botschafts,* laughing to myself and reminiscing about my childhood. We were just an ordinary, happy-go-lucky family who had a talented mom, able to turn everyday occurrences into entertaining stories. Because Mom has such a crowd of *Botschaft* fans, I decided to share these memories with them.

A very special thanks to Mom for letting me use her letters.

—Becky

Megtolsm

Contents

Introduction

Following are a selection of weekly journal entries by Linda Byler that were previously published in *Die Botschaft* newspaper of Lancaster, Pennsylvania. The newspaper publishes weekly community reports from many scribes who tell of happenings in their respective areas and communities.

However, Linda Byler has a special touch to writing and relaying her community's (Newburg, Pennsylvania) news with an added flavor and extra color.

Now, in book form, are special selections from *Die Botschaft* columns that appeared from 1991-1997 for all to enjoy. And—this isn't the "normal" *Botschaft* column.

The Shrinking Rocker

Would the Spigot Explode?

On New Year's Day we traveled to Gettysburg with Dad Bylers to visit *Doddy* Bylers (Sam and Lydia). We took dinner along and *Mommy* had delicious Christmas cookies and candy for us. I always enjoy visiting there. I guess maybe their home reminds me of *Doddy* Weavers back home in Wayne County, Ohio. Is there anything more fascinating to young children than the home of their grandparents? I remember the artesian well in the pasture and the endlessly running water and always the fascination of wondering if the spigot would actually explode if you closed it. And a crow that talked and an open stairway with a corner halfway up where we sat to color in our coloring book. And I remember the bathroom door had a window that was bumpy. It let in the light, but no one could see in. I thought surely the person who invented that was smart! And *Doddy* Weaver had such white hair and a big nose with lots of purple veins on it and he was so kind. Such precious memories etched on young hearts and when we are older, they are golden indeed! We do have a blessed heritage, to have older people among us to respect and learn from.

[JANUARY 3, 1991]

Gardening Glib

Seed catalogs are arriving in the mail already. Thinking of starting a new garden again makes me sigh, but no doubt by the time spring is here I'll be anxious to make the best of it. We did spread mushroom mulch and manure where we intend to have the garden, but that's only the beginning. I suppose I'll be battling those tough alfalfa roots for awhile, and they are enough to try anyone's patience. That's when I'm tempted to buy all my vegetables at Petersheims. If only they'd taste better, huh? I guess we're spoiled with our own fresh garden produce.

[JANUARY 3, 1991]

Hello, Pie Pro

Crist King sei Lizzie: The subject of Boston cream pie was brought up recently, and Gid always says he has never eaten any as good as yours. He claims Crist and he would eat a whole one and they were simply delicious. It's a little hard on my pride that mine aren't as good, so I usually tell him he was younger, worked harder, and was hungrier. So sometime, if you don't mind, would you share the recipe in your column? And I'll decide if they really are as good as he remembers!

[JANUARY 3, 1991]

Jaunty Skater

Our puddle is frozen solid down at the pasture, so on New Year's I took my skates and joined Laura and Andy. I felt a little jaunty and planned on showing the children how well Mom can skate. Well, it was a very humbling experience. First I discovered that I can't stand on one skate while getting into the other one. My arms were flailing and I hollered for someone to help me. So off I went, and it was fun to be on skates, but so sobering and almost humiliating that the ice kept breaking and the children could catch me without too much effort. They tried not to show it, but were relieved when I got my shoes on and walked up the road to the house. Oh well, time waits on no one and we wouldn't want it any different. Every part of our lives has its own blessing. So let us continue on and pray for each other. With the new year being here and the talk of war, we just don't know what the future holds, but we know it is all in God's hands.

[JANUARY 3, 1991]

Little People

Another mild evening after two lovely, sunshiny days. I took baby Rosanne out for her first stroll over the gravel drive and down to the barn, where she met our three ducks and petted Andy's tame pigeon and said hello to the heifers and the horses.

Then we walked across the road to *Doddy* Byler's pasture and said hello to the goat herd. So many fascinating things. She seemed almost bewildered when we got back to the house.

I was baby-sitting today for some little "persons," while their mothers went for a day of visiting schools in the area. Mary Blank and her daughters and daughters-in-law and also Marion Byler. They all looked happy when they returned and said they thoroughly enjoyed their day. That's always inspiring for both teachers and visitors and we should just do it more often.

[JANUARY 29, 1991]

Limb Attacks

Little James Stoltzfus suffered two burned hands last week after misjudging the distance to the hot pallet shop stove. He had blisters on his palms and all of his fingers. He must have really gone through a lot of pain. Eva applied lard and flour, and she said she really has faith in that old remedy.

So our four-year-old, Anna, and I packed a coloring book, a key chain, and some candy hearts, and after doing Monday's wash, we went on our little errand to find James running around happily with his hands all healed except for about two small blisters. While Eva cleaned hats and suits, we had a good old Monday chat just like we always had at home. Time just doesn't erase some things. It only seems to strengthen the bonds between loved ones.

I ran up to Mom long enough to ask her what's wrong with my palm tree. Its leaves are dying and it's covered with a sticky substance. Mom's verdict was mites. She said to throw it out or my other plants would get them. So tonight I had to get rid of it, though it really spites me, as it was so pretty.

[JANUARY 29, 1991]

Interesting Fish Sandwich

Gid thought the children and I would enjoy going to Greencastle Livestock Market, so we all ventured out and sat in very uncomfortable seats under a very, very noisy loudspeaker, selling hundreds of cows that looked exactly alike to me except some were black and some weren't.

The most interesting part of the evening was my fish sandwich at the lunch stand. But I really did enjoy the market and was glad I went. You can always learn something. They were selling for $70. I thought, "My, that's really cheap as big as they are already." Later Gid told me that meant by the pound.

[FEBRUARY 12, 1991]

Shrinking Rocker?

Elmer Fisher sei Lydia had a quilting for the Kauffman aunts and nieces. A day I had looked forward to, and I enjoyed the conversation and food. These quiltings are starting to make my hickory rocker seem to shrink. Or is it because it sets in front of our Surdiac coal stove and it actually is shrinking? The hardwood floor boards in front of the stove are drying out, so there's always a possibility! Anyway, it's time the lawn mower and the flower beds, garden weeding, etc. take care of the "shrinking" hickory rocker.

John Fisher sei Lena had a comfort knotting for "relief" on Wednesday. Joe Blank sei Maryann picked us up with Lady and the buggy, and away we went, all squashed together with comforts and children. I really enjoyed the day. It's so special to get together with friends again, since church is divided. Lena had chocolate mint brownies for coffee break and delicious lasagna for dinner.

The day was much too short, as I had to leave at 1:00 to take Anna to the doctor. She had been constantly complaining of an earache. I expected an infection, but she had lots of hard wax which they washed out with an ear syringe.

[MARCH 13, 1991]

Big as Dinosaurs

The other evening Andy said Gid needs me outside, so I quickly grabbed a sweater and ran out with my bedroom slippers on. He wanted to plow the garden with a walking plow and two huge prancing horses. There was a cold wind blowing and I was shivering and wondering what to do. He asked if I can drive the horses. With my teeth chattering and looking at those big horses (they looked as big as dinosaurs), I said maybe I could guide the plow. Gid told me to just drive them in a straight line, which I proceeded to try to do. The "straight" line looked like a question mark and Gid stopped the horses, sighed, and looked over to Dad Bylers and wondered when Emanuel would come home from work. (If he would have said what he felt like.) Anyway, we gave it another try and once we had a furrow, the one horse knew where to go and things kept improving. We must have been quite a sight, with Andy running along giving advice. After a while it sank in that I was supposed to help plow the whole garden, and I mentioned to Gid that I had my bedroom slippers on. He snorted and looked disgusted, and I kept on going till there was only a thin strip to plow anymore and I had to walk on the plowed earth. And yes, I lost my bedroom slipper about the time Andy announced, "Dad, you should see all the fishworms!" Quite a thrill, and I'm beginning to understand why people love farming. There's just something about tilling the soil that makes you feel a part of nature and close to the earth and our Creator.

The next morning Ellie, our white Percheron mare, gave birth to a colt. He's black with a white star and really big and heavy. The steers were in their pen, chewing their cuds and looking so contented, and a duck sat on a nest of eggs, and pigeons cooed from the rafters. And it was a cozy feeling down there in the barn. We named the colt Abner.

Ben and Marion plan to move on Saturday to their new home. John and Lydia Stoltzfus will soon move in then, and I'm looking forward to having them for neighbors. (At least our garden is plowed.)

[MARCH 13, 1991]

You Said Hunting?

On Easter Monday we traveled to Bedford County to a widower, William Moon, for a visit. He lives at the foot of the mountain, in total privacy, with a creek winding along in back of his old house. His wife died two years ago, and his daughters are married and the youngest one in college, so he always appreciates visits. Dad Bylers have known him for years, but Gid just started to hunt there a few years, ago. Dad butchered a goose, Mom made roast, and I made a kettle of mashed potatoes and also took corn and three pies, as he is so fond of homemade fruit pies.

Gid persuaded us to climb to the top of the mountain where he goes hunting. Bill had to ferry us across the creek with his tractor and wagon. It was so cold and windy, and I looked up to the top of this huge mountain and just sighed inwardly. But I desperately wanted to be a good sport, so off we all went. It was breathtaking, and the only thing that really kept me going was determination to keep up with Gid and never admit how tired I was. I even imagined I could feel for those women that were captured by Indians and made to walk for days and days. I felt like they must have! We drank water from two different springs and there were numerous deer trails, etc. I still can't imagine why men go hunting. About the only way I would enjoy it is if I had a good book to read and plenty of sandwiches to eat.

On the way home we stopped in Needmore to see our colt's daddy. What a truly beautiful horse! He's dapple gray and lives in a rolling pasture, and when he lifts his head, it almost takes your breath away, he's so huge. I'm glad I don't have to plow the garden with him.

[APRIL 10, 1991]

Pilgrims Making Their Way

The sun is shining and a warm breeze is blowing in through the screen door, while bumblebees hum on the porch and the birds are all singing this morning.

I have been baking chocolate chip cookies this morning and want to take some over to Ike Kings.

North district had communion yesterday and ordained a minister, with Ike King (Seth's John's) being the chosen one. His wife is Gid's sister Sarah (Eli Byler's), and my thoughts have been with them this morning. I know it must take much giving up on their part, but my heart is grateful again that we live among men who humble themselves to take this task upon them.

The way to heaven is long and rough, and we need these servants of God. It reminds me of pilgrims making their way along a rocky path, and just when we are most discouraged, a minister refreshes us with a cool drink of water or a piece of bread.

Our church services were held in the home of David and Sarah Flaud, with Ike Stoltzfus having the first part and Ben Kurtz the Old Testament story.

[APRIL 26, 1991]

Little Canine

Ben Esh sei Barbie had buddies' day this week. We all worked outside—raking, mowing, trimming, mulching, and planting some geraniums and shrubs. What an enjoyable day for all of us! Such a delicious dinner, with French rhubarb pie for dessert. John Fisher sei Lena and I walked down the hill and over to their farm to see their litter of Border collie puppies. I'm not a dog lover, but I knew Gid and the children would love to have one, so we picked out a little girl puppy. Anna carried it up the hill and John's little Christy was walking beside her. After a while he said, "Oh, we still have a whole bunch yet," as if assuring himself that it was alright for Anna to have one of his puppies. So, as is the usual story for children with a new puppy, they were delighted and named her Gertie, then Katie and Princess, and her latest name is Lassie. And she is adorable. I even pet her and hold her and I hardly ever pet dogs.

[APRIL 26, 1991]

Sold!

Our annual Amish school sale will be May 11 this year, being held at Jacob Flauds. This is a day we look forward to every year. There's just something about school sales that are special. All the good food and watching the quilts sell, rejoicing with the one whose quilt brings a good price. And meeting lots of old and new acquaintances. Since our children attend the Mennonite school, we don't have too much to do with this sale, but still appreciate and enjoy it every year.

[APRIL 26, 1991]

Duckling Mortality

We had a duck with 23 ducklings this spring, and much to Andy's disappointment, they all died but three. He looked at Gid the other evening and said, "*Ach*, Dad, I guess we're just not too good at raising ducks." What does happen to baby ducks that just disappear? Our banty hens' mortality rate isn't much better, so maybe we have rats in the barn or something.

[APRIL 26, 1991]

Painting What?

Another sunshiny warm day is approaching; no sound this morning but the birds and the neighbor's tractor. The children are all sound asleep, and I was up earlier than usual to make a double batch of cinnamon rolls for a lady who's having a Tupperware party.

We want to paint more fence today, although I haven't broken that news to Laura and Andy yet. No wonder Tom Sawyer got all the neighbor boys to do it. What is more boring than painting board fence?

And we have about twelve rows of corn to hoe, which probably won't thrill them more than fence painting!

Otterbein has their school picnic today, and Dad Bylers want to take our three oldest along. They're looking forward to watching the ball game.

[MAY 22, 1991]

Forget about Geography

Betty had an old school newspaper when I taught school at Otterbein, and it was very interesting, with letters, poems, etc. from pupils who are now married with children of their own. So I had a nice stroll down memory lane yesterday. I got a lump in my throat sometimes, remembering how I had all these upper grade boys and they never caused any serious problems. Did I ever thank them for their respect and cooperation? I doubt it, and if any of my pupils read this, thank you for all the memories.

I'll never forget all we did together—the baseball games, sled riding, and story time when the book was just too interesting to even think of starting our geography.

[MAY 22, 1991]

Pony Express

Gid bought the children a new black pony this week, and it seems we have a really *chite* one. They drive it all over the place and fuss and argue and holler, "Whoa! Whoa!" all the time, and this pony is so unbelievably sweet and patient. I was just shaking with laughter at my kitchen window to see them load and unload, then cautiously pull out, leaning forward as far as they could to be sure and hold the reins right, all telling each other to be careful, and this pony looks as fat and harmless as a kitten.

But it does pay to use caution, as I remember being dumped off a pony cart more than once as a child and the pony running home. We would come after it, crying as we went. When we lived in Reistville in Lebanon, we had a blind old pony named Dolly. When we were six or seven old, we would go to Ben Lantz's with her for milk.

All went very well until a dog jumped out and frightened her so badly that she shied and dumped Eva and me off. What a feeling that was! We were close to our neighbor's electric fence and I thought it was the end of me.

[MAY 22, 1991]

Do You Know Me?

The community was grieved by the death of one of our beloved *diener*, Ike Stoltzfus, who died in Mexico while undergoing an operation. This news was so unexpected and quite a blow to accept, as I'm sure it was for the family.

While at the funeral different people spoke to me about reading these *Botschaft* letters, and I always appreciate encouragement, but I'm getting a little worried. I'm starting to feel like I am somebody, I think. I have often found in my lifetime that about the time I'm starting to think I'm doing pretty good, I fall hard. I feel a bit like a hypocrite, because I'm really not a very nice person at all. My dear husband knows all my shortcomings and would gladly send anyone a list! Perhaps the most spiritual worth for me would be a letter of discouragement, as I do seriously fear of walking with a proud spirit. My letters probably sound like I am a nice, friendly person, and in truth, I am not always.

[SEPTEMBER 24, 1991]

Traveling Jealousies

Dads and Amoses are planning a trip to Kentucky on Thursday morning, and I'm trying so hard to be a good sport and not care one bit, wishing them a safe and happy trip, but in all honesty I'm so jealous I can hardly stand it. I love to travel and see things and new places, so it's not easy to see them go, because just like a six-year-old, I want to go along. So I'll act my 33 years and realize I have three schoolchildren to send off to school, and everything is by far the smoothest when we're all here together.

Dad and Mom Byler have a trip planned to go to Lawrence County next month to their quilt auction. I have never been to Lawrence County where Dad's uncles live and am naturally curious to see where they live and would enjoy seeing where Dad lived as a small boy. But we'll just wave them goodbye, too, as we aren't planning on going along. Gid is a home person (except for hunting) and it's a very good thing I'm married to him or I'd always be on the road.

[SEPTEMBER 24, 1991]

Favorite Season

A beautiful evening with the sun setting behind the mountain in a reddish golden glow, with a flock of mallard ducks flying low across the treetops. My favorite season is here, with warm, woolly socks, apples and cider and fresh pumpkin pie, lovely days, cool nights, and gorgeous colors on the mountain and in the woods.

Israel's Anna is here to spend the night with Laura, and I put my two good maids to washing dishes, while I escaped to plant tulips that *Mommy* Kauffman gave me. I was outside working till almost too dark to see, and have more work for tomorrow evening. I actually believe our newly planted shrubs all survived the summer's drought, and that hickory shredded bark mulch is probably the biggest factor in keeping them moist at the roots.

[OCTOBER 9, 1991]

Oh, Gravity

And I fell! I seriously fell out of Lorna Yoder's van, with the hem of my dress catching on the arm of the seat. We stopped for apples at Horst's Orchards and I quickly got up and the next I remember I was flying through the air and landed very hard, flat on my stomach. I sat up and gasped and moaned and groaned for my breath, and Frances Horst came running and started to pat my back. Now that I think back, it seems Mom and Lorna were a little dense. They just sat in the van staring out the window, asking if I was alright. No, I certainly was not alright, but I undoubtedly would survive, and my pride was just hurt bad enough that I actually felt like crying.

My one elbow was all scraped up and bruised and I hurt all over for a few days. I couldn't wait to show Gid my serious injuries, and he looked concerned for a few seconds, then burst out laughing. I was so insulted, I told him he's very lucky I didn't break my arm because at that moment, watching him wash dishes would have been a lovely sight.

[OCTOBER 9, 1991]

A Strenuous Time

I had a few lonely days this week, with Mom Byler at work at John Petersheim's store and John sei Lydia in Lancaster with her parents for a few days. I miss Lydia but am sure she is enjoying every minute with her family.

I never stay lonely for long, as it seems there's always someone dropping in to say hello.

Today a former neighbor's son, Edwin Caudill, came to visit after being in San Diego, California, for his basic training for the Navy. He's a quiet, respectful boy of eighteen and it was so interesting to hear his story. They really experience something through those two months of training. They ran or marched 600 miles total in two months' time, and their final test is to do 60 push-ups and 55 sit-ups in two minutes. Then they immediately run $1^1/_2$ miles in ten minutes. It made me tired all over to imagine such strenuous exercise. Now he goes to school in California while in the Navy and will perhaps not see his parents for close to a year. He said he was extremely homesick the first few weeks, but the toughest part is over now. Our thoughts will certainly be with him through the coming year.

[OCTOBER 9, 1991]

Later Ventures

Tuesday was the wedding of Sam King and Lovina Kurtz, given together in marriage by Uncle Jacob Stoltzfus of Maryland. They had a beautiful sunshiny day, almost as if it was made to order, and we wish them the Lord's blessings. We helped make roast along with Israels and Mose Hostetlers. I enjoyed it more than last year. I even cut off the feet and cleaned the gizzards, but so far I have never ventured inside a chicken with my hand. Perhaps when I'm 40 I might be brave enough. Who knows?

[OCTOBER 26, 1991]

This Man I Can't See

Last week I had the privilege of meeting a lady, who on first impression just reminded me of being a "little rough around the edges," but I noticed her eyes kept searching mine and she seemed so wise and knowing. In the course of the evening she told me that 21 years ago, she left her husband, with her four children and $17 in her pocket, not knowing her destination or her future. Her husband abused the children, and when she stopped a butcher knife going across the table at her thirteen-year-old son, she knew the time had come to leave, as quickly as possible. They existed on $20.50 a week.

Being Amish and as family oriented as we are, my first question was, "Where were your parents?" Her mother was sick and poor in Lewistown and her father had died.

She continued, "Everyone tells me I need a man, but I have a Man. This Man I can't see, but He comes so close I can almost feel Him. I talk to Him like I talk to you, and He cares about me. I don't know why, there's nothing I do to deserve it. That Man is the Lord."

She spoke with so much conviction that my heart thrilled to hear her words. But immediately I felt deeply ashamed for having judged her when I first met her. How often do we unknowingly measure sparsely other people's cups?

For with what measure ye mete, it shall be measured to you again. I felt her faith was so much greater than my own, and how important that our white coverings and long dresses are for real, and we have faith to match and works to follow.

[OCTOBER 26, 1991]

Humor Is Good

Lots of different people inquired about my elbow, and if I was healthy again. I'm fine and my arm is usable, but the elbow is still very sore and touchy. I hope I don't appear like a silly person, or like one always trying to be funny. I enjoy other people's sense of humor, and humor sometimes puts the oil on the rusty patches of life. I mean, life just isn't all roses. We have our sorrows, struggles, and frustrations, and our faith is the most important—to actually trust the Lord Jesus in all our situations—but sometimes humor is necessary to take things in stride.

[OCTOBER 26, 1991]

Sew Askew

Dad Bylers returned home safely from Lawrence County on Saturday evening. It was so nice to see them come home. Everything seemed lonely in their house when I went to borrow (steal?) some green thread. The goats all stood in the pasture and baaed and maaed (or whatever goats say) on Saturday, so they must have been homesick for Dad.

Last evening the children and I walked out to Alvin Fisher sei Anna. She makes nighties and sleepers, sheet sets, comforters, etc. for a very reasonable price. I was pleased with my purchases and am always so grateful for her store. They are planning on moving in Samuel Lantz's shop, for a larger facility. I mean, move Samuel's shop over to their place.

Sewing is not my favorite job. I don't know why. I am totally left-handed, and I have only one speed... and that's full-speed-ahead, and I always end up feeling cross-eyed, my hair sticking out, and my cap askew, and can't wait to sweep and close the sewing machine. Our talents are all different.

[OCTOBER 26, 1991]

The Ugly Quilt

Winter Work and Fun

We're having lovely winter weather with some snow and plenty of ice for the skaters. I was so excited about our three or four inches of snow, but that evening when I went to the wash house and there were wet coats, mittens, boots, socks, and scarves all over the place, I wondered why I wished for snow. Rosanne was on the back porch scooping up mittened handfuls of snow, eating it as fast as she could and her eyes were a picture of pure delight.

Long winter days and it still seems the weeks fly by just as fast as they do in the summertime. Plenty of quiltings, buddies' days, etc. to keep us all going.

Florence King had a quilting on Tuesday, planning on doing four quilts in two days. She had a good turnout the first day with about the right amount of ladies, so we all had work. Our group felt quite pleased with ourselves as we finished ours around three o'clock when our driver came. And we even talked a lot, although I didn't say near as much as I usually do!

Yesterday Mom Kauffman, Eva, and Ruthie were here and we put in the quilt I had appliquéd this winter. I pressed all the seams and tried to show Mom how neat it looked and told her, "Isn't it something?" She just snorted and looked totally unimpressed and told me you shouldn't praise yourself.

Ruthie was so tired and sleepy from skating until 11:30 the previous evening at Elmer Fisher's, and Eva had to go help clean the schoolhouse, and I thought everybody seemed kind of grouchy. Finally I said I wish they would all go home early so I could take a nap.

Mom brought a big kettle of homemade chicken potpie for dinner and Eva claimed she put perfume in it. It tastes funny. Mom said she did put saffron in it, but it was all Eva's notion, I believe, because it was good. Oh well, the next time they want to help quilt, Ruthie should get her sleep and we should all feel more *fleisich.* It's just the way sisters are.

[JANUARY 30, 1992]

Sanity Assured

A cold windy evening, after a surprise snowstorm yesterday. Snow swirled from the northwest accompanied by strong gusts of wind.

I had started housecleaning upstairs on Tuesday, and Wednesday morning there was a dusting of snow on the ground and it was a bit windy, but nevertheless I thought, well, I'll just dig in and finish that upstairs. So, with not much thought to the weather, I proceeded to throw comforts, quilts, curtains, rugs, and all that goes with "cleaning fever" to the wash house and soon had my trusty air motor going full tilt, wash machine stuffed with thick comforts, and plenty of soap. My mind was on a one-track rhythm, *Get that wash out and get started upstairs.*

Well, to make a long story short, the snow came down in earnest, and the wind kept getting stronger, and I kept telling myself that it's only a spring *shtivva* and will soon be over. By ten o'clock I was afraid to look out at the washline, till five-year-old Anna said, "Mom, there is a quilt and an apron blowing away." The comforts were down, the line was sagging from the poles bending, and I accepted the fact that I had just done something extremely stupid.

About the time I wrestled the comforts in, my good friend, Jane Reiff, came and didn't say anything—she just stood at the bottom of the stairs with her eyebrows raised a few inches. I think she was seriously questioning my sanity—to see these comforts dripping all over my hardwood floor and the rest of my wash scraping along the ground in a blizzard. I had to assure her that I was still alright. She generously offered to take me to the laundromat, and I accepted gladly and will forever be in her debt, as I was quite grateful to bring home the dry folded clothes.

I'll never tell her I had to scrape off the ice to put my screens in! Needless to say, supper that evening was potato soup and hot dogs, and Gid was very nice and didn't say anything.

[MARCH 12, 1992]

Now Don't You...

We had the pleasure of meeting Eli Dad's uncle, Rudy Kurtz of Lawrence County, last evening. It was very interesting to visit with him, but I can't say too much more, because every time he would launch his stories he would look straight at me and say, "Now don't you put this in *Die Botschaft!*" But he did relate many an interesting story of his younger years and we were an appreciative audience.

[MARCH 12, 1992]

Counting Chicks Yet?

The children had an interesting project in school, when Jay Stauffer brought an incubator and let everyone have two eggs to hatch. It was a source of endless discussions around the table, with Andy saying he thinks Edith's chickie was only resting. Laura told him in no uncertain terms that when a chickie lies on its back with its feet straight up in the air it is positively dead. And Becky's supposedly rotten egg produced a beautiful little black chickie, which was a pure miracle, because they thought it was rotten.

Quite interesting and helps the February humdrums for the children.

[MARCH 12, 1992]

Of Housecleaning and Blizzards

Today found us four girls over in Mom Kauffman's house with all good intentions of housecleaning it for her before they get home. They left on Tuesday with Jake Flauds and Steve Stoltzfuses on a trip to various places and to Florida. We all miss them and are looking forward to their return. We got all the cleaning done, but it kept all four of us busy, talking and laughing. We made up a poem for Dad and Mom to read when they get home, and between us, I thought it was a fairly good piece of poetry, till we couldn't find a word to rhyme with trip. The whole day had a hilarious ending.

We're still sticking to our two-mile walk every evening, although with these days of housecleaning and all, I feel quite exhausted by evening. Through rain and snow and cold winds, we faithfully keep walking. John sei Lydia and I were so cold this evening, we were seriously considering long johns for tomorrow evening. What a joy to come into a warm bright kitchen with Laura baking Grandpa cookies, and little Rosanne so glad to see me come home. Sometimes we have so very many blessings in simple homey things; all we need to do is stop every once in a while and just appreciate it all. Home is precious—blizzards, wet comforts, and all.

[MARCH 12, 1992]

The Old White Mare

Warm breezes assure us that winter's blast can't be too serious in April and spring is on its way. Lots of seeds are being planted, lawn mowers are finding their way out of sheds, etc.

Our garden seeds are all safely planted in neat rows through my new garden. This unexpected warmth really brought out the planting fever, but how to get the garden ready with our black Percherons in Lawrence County? Gid hitched up Ellie, the white mare, our source of discussions for awhile already. How many of you wives know the feeling of, "I said all I'm going to say, and if you want to feed her and haul the manure...fine!" End of subject. Anyway, Ellie decided this is ridiculous and took off. Knocking over two fence posts and dodging the clothesline, she galloped around the corner of the barn, fell, and slid a few yards on the road, before she came to rest by the barn. I was on my walk, but all the girls came running to relate this scene quite breathlessly. So Lydia and I stood in the middle of the road and decided we're out of patience; we'll call Dewalt, a man who does gardens with a small tractor and rototiller. The next evening found Mr. Dewalt happily at work and us all out planting the garden, but alas! When the time came to pay, his fee was $74! My, I was speechless, but said, "Gid, Gid, do you have any cash?" And the good husband answered, "You got him; you pay him," which I humbly proceeded to do. I squeaked out a tiny little "thank-you" and if I would have been a rabbit, my ears would have hung straight down. I was so humbled and humiliated. Later I asked Gid why it cost so much and he said that's an expensive piece of equipment and he can't run it for nothing. Old Ellie keeps looking better and better. Oh, such is life when you lack patience and don't have too much common sense.

[APRIL 9, 1992]

Quilting, Eating, and Talking

I'm tired tonight and a little grouchy. My eyes are crossed because I quilted a lot today and ate too much carrot cake with cream cheese icing. Mom, Eva, and Ruthie were here all day and we really got a lot accomplished. We were all in a good mood. There was no chicken potpie with perfume in it this time, and we thoroughly enjoyed each other's company.

Marion had sisters' day on Tuesday for us Byler sisters, a day I enjoyed too. I so seldom get to Bens and was nice to have Joe Fisher sei Mary and David Byler sei Emma with us. We sewed on different projects and talked all day.

Last Wednesday, I helped David Flaud sei Sarah with her quilt. Just the two of us and our youngest children, and it was a peaceful day. We hardly even stopped to eat lunch, we were so busy quilting, and I do believe we covered every subject from husbands to drivers. So many verses and little sentences about friends, and they're all true. Friends are precious in this sad old world, with its ups and downs. They are priceless, and true friendship makes hearts light.

[APRIL 9, 1992]

Big Money

Well, everyone is asleep but me, and I would probably feel best by joining them in their slumbers. Andy is at Dad Kauffmans this evening. He went giggling with Jr. and wants to go to Carlisle to the special Easter sale to sell some of his pigeons. He was walking as tall as he possibly could this evening, and his eyes looked like two blue pictures of happiness. He even tucked in his chin and tried to talk low, which is befitting to a person who has $5 to buy his own lunch and sell six pigeons.

And Becky was allowed to go home with Paul, to Israels, which resulted in half a dozen leaps, skips, and jumps. The exuberance of youth! It makes me tired to think of it, so I will retire for the night.

[APRIL 9, 1992]

Optimistic Bylers

Mom Byler was mowing yard and I should have been doing it too, but I'll tackle it tomorrow evening. I always enjoy outside work, by far my favorite, but my yard seriously gives me the blues this spring. We planted 100% Kentucky bluegrass two years ago and with two dry summers it has lots of bare spots, then tufts of grass, and my reel mower bounces over it, making miserable mowing. And the dandelions and all other sorts of healthy-looking weeds are doing absolutely great. So I will mow everything and pretend it's just a nice green carpet.

The True Value owner in town said to apply Turf Builder in late May, but can I stand these healthy weeds that long? Gid is the most optimistic person I ever saw. He always assures me by next spring all these bare spots will be covered with grass and I just nod my head and try hard to believe him. Gid's mom is just as bad, *gel,* Mom? She always says, "It'll come, Linda." It's almost a joke for us. Patience, patience, patience, and lots of faith.

[APRIL 23, 1992]

Chastisement for the Unknown

Do you ever get the feeling the Lord is punishing you for some misdeed? Like you bite your tongue so awful hard after being grouchy or something?

Well, last week I'm sure I did something way wrong because I was certainly chastened. First I cut my finger on a knife in my dishwater, which caused much unhandiness and misery. The next day I mowed my "beautiful green grass," bounce, bounce, bounce, with the results being one grand blister which popped open in the palm of my hand. Ouch! Washing dishes, combing my girls' hair, washing laundry—everything frustrated me. Then I was quilting with an old thimble, because I couldn't find my good one. Then the needle slipped and went straight up my thumbnail. My, that hurt! Five minutes later I was thinking, *Wouldn't it be awful if that happened again?* And you know what? It did! Exactly the same thumb, except further in than before. I stood up and jerked my quilt frame away and actually thought I would pass out.

So whatever I did wrong, I'm duly chastened. Everything is healed nice and all is forgiven.

[APRIL 23, 1992]

Tasty Blanket

A dark overcast day, with a strong wind blowing in from the east, accompanied by rain and cool temperatures. I'm thinking of our school sale tomorrow which is to be held at Jake Flauds. We're all looking forward to it, especially the children, but if this weather persists, I had better clean some coats and warm clothes. I always enjoy the food and meeting old friends. And isn't it exciting to sell a quilt you made? The first year I sold a quilt, my heart went too fast and beat so hard, and the higher the auctioneer went, the harder I chewed on my baby's blanket!

[MAY 8, 1992]

School's Out—Now What?

I've just finished my Friday cleaning, and the children came home from school at 9:30 with their report cards. I wish I could report their youthful glee and happiness that school's out! But to be perfectly honest, I think it *spites* them. Laura sat on the couch and didn't have much to say, and Becky paged through her old artwork and books and didn't look thrilled at all. Andy took off for the barn and his beloved pigeons, and has been hammering ever since, but he did announce that he wishes school wasn't over. Now, am I a poor mother? Do my children have a rough home life, or what? I must admit, it makes me feel strangely inferior when they don't relish the prospect of a summer at home with good old Mom.

But perhaps I'll just give special honor to teacher Marianne, and a good school with plenty of loving friends. It has always been that way; our children just love to go to school. And I suppose that in itself is a blessing. Finally I told them we'll usually quickly do our work this summer then go to the creek to swim and take a picnic lunch, roast hot dogs, etc., which didn't get much response either. Oh well, they'll just have to put up with me now!

[MAY 8, 1992]

Muddy Fishing

Ben Byler said on Sunday he's been wanting to talk to me for awhile. He thinks I should write this in *Die Botschaft*—David Byler went trout fishing in the creek at Rowe Run in Pinola. He caught a fine trout and was leaning over with his net, when he slipped off the bank, going headfirst into the water. He was wearing hip-waders and there was deep mud on the bottom. Ben looked over and he was paddling the water, completely soaked, trying to get out of his calamity!

I suppose he got out okay 'cause they were here at church and he looked normal and happy.

Jimmy said he was fishing in the same creek, and jumped onto a partly submerged log, slipped and fell, sitting down into deep gooey black mud, up to his waist. I really wish I could have seen him. Maybe these young men should take up another hobby, like gardening or mowing the lawn, instead of sitting in mud.

. . . . . .

Well, the children are in and hungry for lunch. Becky said, "Mom, are we going to have tomato soup for lunch every day the whole summer long?" They are just sure they must work like slaves in the garden and live on tomato soup. So I will see if I can find something that gives them all a brighter outlook for the future.

[MAY 8, 1992]

Two Andys?

We're invited to Dad Kauffmans for supper this evening. Everyone is all excited, taking baths and finding shoes, etc. Then comes Mom's job of combing four girls. Seems when we go away, it simply takes time to comb everyone, but with Andy, it seems so simple to run a brush through his hair and he's ready. Oh well, I wouldn't want to give up one of my girls, and more often than not, I wonder with some misgivings, how would it be to have two Andys?

The girls all play peacefully together, doll or school or whatever, then along comes Andy, just like a summer storm on someone's picnic. This week he crept outside the playhouse, yowling like a cat, and I could just imagine the girls chose to ignore him, hoping he'd go away. Well, the yowls became louder and louder, until I was ready to put a stop to it, when the playhouse door burst open with three furious girls, two to chase Andy and one to come tattle. Oh, then the wisdom to always know what to do! Scold Andy, or just tell the girls to bear with him, he needs attention and companionship too sometimes. As soon as Gid comes home in the evening, peace is restored, because Andy is an absolute disciple of Gid's, of which I am always thankful for. I've often told Andy if he did have a brother, he'd have to share his dad.

[MAY 21, 1992]

Wounded Pride

Our school sale went well, with the rain clearing up in the forenoon and sunshine the rest of the day. The quilts sold well, and some of the crafts and wall hangings were above average. My appliquéd quilts sold rather low and it was a little hard on my pride. I mostly received $500 or more for mine, but it seemed these just didn't appeal to anyone or something. I came home in the evening with two of Bena's chocolate shooflies and drowned my sorrows with them.

[MAY 21, 1992]

Radish Abundance

As everyone knows, I'm a failure at lots of things, like growing lima beans, having patience, etc., but I must relate my radish story. We planted an ounce of red and one of white with the seeder, and I believe every radish sprouted and grew. We had radishes by the gallon. I gave them away, and we had radishes every meal except for breakfast. There were three short rows remaining, so I told the children to pull them all and clean them. Upon arriving home I simply laughed. They had my largest stainless steel mixing bowl heaped as high as possible and a whole bunch thrown on the compost heap when they simply got too tired of cleaning them.

I almost felt like that story in the reading book of the family who owned the magic pot that wouldn't stop boiling. I'm also making another effort at lima beans. I waited till the last week in May to plant, and sprinkled lime in the rows, and plan on spraying with Sevin to see if I can elude those little black bugs that eat the new sprouts.

[JUNE 4, 1992]

They Put It Where?!

This week Dad Byler ordered horse feed from Agway and told them to unload it in the small barn, meaning his barn across the road. Guess where they put it? In our phone shanty! Whoever was the driver must have different ideas of small barns than some people.

[JUNE 4, 1992]

Drowning Worms

Probably everyone has things planned because of Monday being *Pingsta.* Well, being Mrs. Gideon Byler usually doesn't include lots of social activities, as my husband is most definitely a loner, while I enjoy crowds and people. But it's kind of growing on me, too. I can much easier just accept it since the children are older, and much to my chagrin, my oldest daughter very much resembles her dad's hermit-like ways! And she sticks up for Gid with, "Let's just stay home, Mom."

On Ascension Day, early in the morning, Gid chirped and sang and tweeted around here, and announced he's going fishing at Bender's pond in Pleasant Hall. Well, I felt like the worst sport, still tired and wanting to sleep, and the idea of sitting in the warm sun drowning worms definitely did not appeal to me. So the little girls and I went to Dad Kauffmans, as their days get long sometimes, too. Mom's couch suited me just fine and I had plenty of appliquéing to keep me occupied. But it turned out that Dads had company all day, off and on. Ike Eshes, with Diesel Dans from the Valley, and his brother (I don't know their names), and the new family that lives with Ikes from Enon Valley came after dinner. Then Uncle Elam Lapps and Emanuel Kauffmans, Benuel Fishers, and Ben Beilers came, and it was nice visiting with everyone. That evening we all regrouped as a family to discuss the day's events.

[JUNE 4, 1992]

Hidden Head

Oh, yes, how could I forget till last to announce the birth of little Aquilla? Joe and Maryann Blank are the happy parents of a little boy, and being neighbors with Joes and all our walks together made it special. He is so cute. He much resembles a little Indian papoose, all round and fat with dark hair. Like Andy said, "There's so much hair you can't even see his head."

[JUNE 4, 1992]

Price of Pleasure

We walked home with Jason Fishers and Levi Kings and they stopped in for a drink before walking on home to Elmers. It was a warm afternoon and Anna was so thirsty, so *Doddy* Kauffmans stopped and they clambered over the wheelchair into the back seat and they dropped them off at home. That evening we were invited to our Mennonite neighbors, Martin Reiffs, for a delicious picnic supper. Sometimes different food tastes so good. And this was no exception. Ham balls, potato salad, deviled eggs, chips, pickles, vegetables with dip and cheese, fruit salad, and bars and different cakes made a very refreshing supper on a warm evening. Eugene Martins, Alan Yoders, and a River Brethren couple who are also good friends, Gerald Gaymans, were invited too.

I feel so smart right now with all our socializing we've been doing. I think Gid is doing very well and I told him on Sunday evening, "Now, isn't this so much better than sitting home every weekend?" He agreed that he really enjoyed it, so we'll see how long our spree lasts!

Last Sunday evening Ben Stoltzfuses, Israels, and Ben Kurtzes were here for supper. We had a long table set up and it was filled with six little ones at the small picnic table and three girls ate on the porch. But I thoroughly enjoyed the evening, and it was fun to cook a big meal for company once again.

Eva made graham cracker fluff and Aunt Sarah brought apple salad, so Monday found me with the worst case of nibbling at all the leftover desserts. I wonder how far you have to walk to walk off a big pile of date pudding.

[JUNE 30, 1992]

Let's Try Cotton

Today I was in town, as Laura had a dentist appointment to have two teeth extracted. She has permanent teeth coming down over her baby teeth, which refused to budge. So hopefully they will now come into their proper space, as it certainly looked as if something should be done.

Where is it more humid and just plain hot than on the streets in town? With black shoes and stockings and a *halsduch,* and then you climb into a van that is hotter yet, and you just sit there and give up and try to be as pleasant as possible. Then someone asks, "Where is my purse?" and you try and be nice and helpful, but you think, *Grrrr!* Why is 90° weather so hard on your good nature?

It felt very good to enter our cool house, and kick shoes and stockings and change into a cotton dress. Why don't we Lancaster people, or whatever we're called, wear dacron and cotton for Sunday? It would definitely be cooler, but perhaps we'd look wrinkled and sloppy. I have a notion to make a cotton cape and apron once and see if someone else will too!

[JUNE 30, 1992]

To Get What?!

I got such a good hearty laugh out of the person who wrote about the little girl who told the salesman her mother went down to the cellar to get fat. I won't mention the name, as this boy is just small, but I couldn't help thinking of this. The gas man came to Israel's door and asked for Eva, and the little boy informed him, "Why, my mom's up in the *spouter*." I never found out if the gas man went outside to search the spouting for Eva or not, but I kind of doubt it.

[JUNE 30, 1992]

Exciting Andy

It's very seldom that any member of our family reads my letters, but Laura read last week's and looked at me so disgustedly and said, "Mom, the only thing you write about is Andy." It does seem that way sometimes, but I told her he's the only exciting thing on South Road sometimes. I don't mean to brag or mention my own children too much though. A mother's life revolves around her children a lot, especially if her husband works away from home, and then I guess naturally you tend to use them as subjects for letter writing material.

They're perfectly human children, with their spats and bossy arguments, but life would be empty without every one of their special ways. And, yes, my garden is nice and clean, and we often eat tomato soup and toasted cheese sandwiches for lunch.

Gid wants to go to Bedford County this evening, and the children are begging to go swimming in the creek. So, I'll see if we have any hot dogs to roast, and we have a cold watermelon in the refrigerator and blueberries Mom gave me, so we'll see how noisy the kitchen gets when I announce it.

[JUNE 30, 1992]

A Green Thumb and A Clean House

Another warm humid day, and a real thunderstorm is brewing in the southwest, and hopefully it will bring a respite from the heat. We've had showers of rain at least every week, and the gardens and yards look like a picture. Corn and hay fields are bright green and growing as fast as possible. And my lima beans! They are simply beautiful, loaded with buds, and I dust them carefully and keep all the weeds out—everything I can think of. I suppose I could sing to them yet, but I certainly have high hopes for a good crop of lima beans.

A busy Friday morning. I woke Laura and Andy early and we worked in the yard—mowing and trimming, cleaning, and hoeing flower beds. When the sun really emerged from behind the clouds, we were headed for the house to do our Friday cleaning. Becky and Anna danced and giggled around the kitchen, collecting the dust mop and furniture polish, rags, and brooms to go clean upstairs to surprise Laura. They had quite a thumping and bumping up there for awhile, and were so proud to announce their secret. Andy is totally unenthused about Friday, as he detests mowing lawn, but had to smile in spite of himself when I sang out that it was Friday morning. Then the pickles were picked and sliced and put into jars for kosher dills, after which we brought the laundry in, folded it and put it away. Now we still have some baking and food fixing to do this evening.

[JULY 17, 1992]

Raspberry Wonders

Ben Stoltzfus sei Mary had buddies' day last week, but I didn't go. I kind of felt like I was playing hooky and it's not that I wouldn't have enjoyed it, but I was tired of putting on a *halsduch* and going away when it's warm. When the temperatures soar into the 90s I can be a real poor sport.

The day before, Mom Kauffman and I went to Juniata County to Menno Peacheys for 80 quarts of raspberries, and we divided them among us girls. They were big and juicy, and I proceeded to cook them as soon as I got home.

My friend Jane stopped in and was astounded that I don't have a juicer or steamer and ran home and got hers, and we put the partially cooked raspberries in there and, wonder of wonders, the kettle boiled and the juice ran neatly into a stainless steel bucket. I decided that's one of the world's greatest inventions and soon had fourteen quarts juice and five batches jelly.

[JULY 17, 1992]

Teary-Eyed Tots

Two little girls are sitting beside me, both in tears. Anna is trying to console herself with her thumb and Rosanne has her tootie, with big shiny tears ready to spill over. Laura, Andy, and Becky are driving Chocolate, our pony, over to *Mommy* Kauffmans to put wood preservative on their patio. They were supposed to go this morning, but they forgot all about it and it's 11:00 already. So they quickly left, causing much sorrow for Anna and Rosanne.

[JULY 29, 1992]

A Real Bee

Andy came up from the barn this morning calmly asking what to put on a bee sting. I gave him something and asked if it was a real bee, and he didn't even cry? No, he said, he just scratched it awhile. Laura and Becky looked up from their cookie baking with these incredulous expressions. Laura said, "It wasn't a real bee." Andy promptly informed her, "It was too and look at this sting." The girls scream and whoop and holler and cry all at once when they get stung. The last time Anna was stung I thought the worst, like a broken leg or something, from the way she sounded. I remember how that used to hurt—tramping on those little white clover flowers in the yard, where there was always at least one bee.

[JULY 29, 1992]

Croquet with Doddy

Emanuel gave *Doddy* Byler a lawn croquet set for Father's Day this year, and that has been quite the thing for our children and *Doddy* already. I do believe they would play for a whole day solid, if they had the chance. Andy gets overenthused and jumps up and down and hollers, and even broke a brand-new croquet mallet when he thumped it on the ground in the frustration of losing.

They always let Becky help too, and she's almost always way behind, but just thoroughly enjoys herself nonetheless. *Doddy* just loves almost any kind of game and our children take advantage of it.

[JULY 29, 1992]

The Other Doddy

Mom Kauffman said last evening she wishes the grandchildren could have known Dad Kauffman when he was still healthy and able. He used to enjoy pitching quotes and playing badminton. It seems like a dream now to think of him ever walking again.

He certainly is not capable of doing much anymore. Last evening Gid and Jr. sat him on an armless chair to get him into the van. He enjoys going to town sometimes, but it gets increasingly harder to take him anywhere. But since Gid needed shoes, we decided to take him along to the mall last evening, or rather Dads asked us to go along.

Gid decided it's easier to lock both arms around his chest, under his arms, and just lift or drag him right out on his wheelchair. Poor Dad, it just tugs at your heart to see it, especially when you see how hard he's trying to be a good sport and it must be humiliating. He lost both bedroom slippers and was laughing about it, and that's when I felt like crying 'cause I pity him so bad. It takes lots of patience and more patience.

[JULY 29, 1992]

Enter Emily

We have been blessed with another daughter who was born at Mollie's in Juniata the third of August. We named her Emily, or rather the girls named her, and she weighed seven pounds and eight ounces. So now I am the mother of five daughters, and Andy still has no brother. He turned ten years old the day before Emily was born and was the only sad spot on this happy occasion. He didn't want anything to do with her the first day, and when he finally held her he just couldn't hide his disappointment, looking at her with the most wishful expression. "Oh, Mom, I wish she was a boy." Needless to say, I swallowed a huge lump in my throat, smiled brightly, and told him God just wants him and Dad to be together or else He would have given us a boy. He's quite happy again, and we're enjoying our little girl immensely. One tiny squeak from the crib and three pairs of feet go pounding across the floor. I told the girls, positively no fighting over this baby, but they still stand around and pinch each other, or make faces at the fortunate one who sits proudly holding her.

Israel's Anna is here this week and she's doing a good job with the corn and just whatever work there is to be done.

[AUGUST 11, 1992]

Boy-Turned-Goose

Gid and Andy went to Leinbachs Auction last Friday evening, and much to Andy's delight, Gid purchased a pair of geese.

For a while I was a little concerned about Andy's good *fashtant.* I think he was a little overwhelmed with these wonderful gee over to walk and flapped his arm honked the most awful honks. He even lay in the sandbox giving himself a goose dust bath, honking all the while. Gid and I sat on the porch and I said, "What is he doing?" Gid was laughing silently till tears ran out of his eyes and finally he told me he's taking a bath.

Andy loves anything that flies or has wings. Birds, ducks, banties, geese, whatever. He has a real zoo of pigeons and doves down in the barn and that's where half of his time is spent.

[AUGUST 11, 1992]

Shopping with a Howling Baby

Our Emily has reached the grand old age of three weeks now. She's a little more fussy than Rosanne was, but not an irritable baby so far. She does not enjoy or appreciate a pacifier which is always more of a problem. My first trip to the Weis Market in town was a total disaster. I took Becky along to help, and when we entered the building, Emily decided this cool temperature and the bright lights are not for her, and started crying. *Oh dear,* I thought, *I hope she takes this pacifier.* Well, she was definitely not in the frame of mind for any "tootie," so I gave her to Becky so

I could continue purchasing my things. Poor Becky! Emily screamed louder, and Becky looked pleadingly at me. People were watching us, so I took her, trying in vain to comfort her. Anyway, I felt exactly like that old reading book story of the man and his son and the donkey, who tried to please everyone, till they ended up carrying the donkey. Finally, after trying to hold her or put her in the seaty or giving her to Becky, I just started throwing groceries into the cart as fast as I could, with Emily screaming as loud as she could. I told the checkout lady that everyone will probably be relieved when I leave, and she didn't say they wouldn't be!

[AUGUST 25, 1992]

Wounded Ego

Our school sale was well attended and we had better profits than previous years. I went for a few hours in the afternoon, just to watch my quilt sell. It was not a pretty quilt, but I didn't get very much for my pretty quilts at the Amish sale so I figured I would make a black quilt with red and green pieced baskets, an old pattern. Well, it only brought $210, so I did not sell it. And much to my embarrassment the auctioneer asked why I wouldn't sell it for that. He said, "There are lots of prettier quilts here that are selling for less." I knew it wasn't pretty, but he didn't have to tell everybody.

So I slunk back to the schoolhouse with my ugly quilt in a garbage bag and stuck it under the bench, sat down on the bench, and pouted. I felt extremely sorry for myself. It was raining and the baby was crying, and I thought of sad things. Like I have ants in my pantry and I should do something about it, and we're not getting any baby cards and I suppose people forgot we have a baby. Even my hoagie didn't have enough mayonnaise on it. The other auctioneer came in and told me kindly that I did the right thing. Those quilts are worth more than that. There just wasn't the right buyer present. That perked me up somewhat. I thought since, perhaps it's just the Lord telling me to take good care of my little girls and forget about making quilts now.

Sure is hard on my pride, though, and that auctioneer didn't have to be so loud.

[AUGUST 25, 1992]

Busheling Limas

Yesterday Mom, Eva, and Ruthie were here to help with my abundant crop of precious lima beans. What a thrill—picking bushels of limas! Twenty-seven pints for the freezer and hopes of another 27.

Sam Katie of North Carolina: Thank you for the advice. I must say, it worked. We enjoyed our first meal last evening, but I'm wondering if lima beans should not be eaten while nursing a tiny baby. Last night was one of not too much sleep, with Emily awake or throwing up or crying.

[AUGUST 25, 1992]

Bountiful Showers

Warm and humid weather with wet foggy mornings. We had a nice rain over the weekend and another shower last evening, accompanied by thunder and lightning. We're still mowing yard once or twice a week, and my lawn mowers and trimming shears are all getting dull from overuse. We have surely been blessed with rains throughout the summer, and our loaded can shelves and stocked freezers attribute to this fact. We decided this summer, it's no wonder Lancaster people are so *worky,* they have to be if it rains!

[SEPTEMBER 9, 1992]

Aging Mama

And with a tired sigh, I must admit having a new baby on August 3, has had its challenges. The corn was ready, lima beans hanging on by the bushels, tomatoes in every corner, and Red Haven peaches were ready. But everything turned out well, with help from good old Mom and sisters. But now that Emily is almost six weeks old, I feel like I'm 60 instead of 34. I suppose I could have twelve children and would never learn that it doesn't pay to be too ambitious too soon. But this week I'm relaxing and sneaking some very good naps throughout the day, so hopefully I will return to age 34 by the end of the week.

[SEPTEMBER 9, 1992]

Faithful Baby-Sitter

My overenthused baby-sitters have had a change of attitude. Emily is just common stuff now. They hold her awhile then, "Who wants her?" All except for faithful Anna, who still sits and rocks her in her little rocking chair.

While stirring pudding at the stove, and baby crying, I hollered out the screen door for Anna. She soon had the baby soothed, and I told her she is simply the best baby-sitter. She slanted me the most endearing expression and said, "Well, Mom, it's no wonder. Don't you know I just love to hold babies?"

Sometimes a bit of praise works wonders. I was wondering to myself if it would work to tell Gid he can fix sewing machine stands better than anyone else, make wonderful porch railing, etc., etc., etc. Aren't there always things husbands have on their someday list?

[SEPTEMBER 9, 1992]

The Joys of Motherhood

While rocking baby Emily this week, I was thinking to myself how tired I was and wondering why you ever want another baby. They take up so much time, and at night you feed them and tiptoe back to bed and at long last drift off to a much-needed sleep when, "Waaaa!" Oh dear! So you burp her and rock her and cast many envious glances at dear sleeping husband and seriously wonder why God created babies to have such a *gamach*. But, oh, the next morning, with the tiny little face next to your own, and I'm scolding her thoroughly, telling her what a naughty baby she is, and she flashes a smile of pure delight, your heart melts with the most precious feeling, and all of a sudden everything makes sense again. Their time of innocence is so short, and soon they will be going to school and you wonder where the time went.

It is a serious responsibility, this raising children, and more so than young parents like us realize. But what a joy to trust the good Lord to help us as trials come along, for He will not give us more than He gives us the strength to carry on.

. . . . .

No Andy stories this week. He has safely returned to school and is busy with his pigeons and rabbits in the evening.

[SEPTEMBER 9, 1992]

A Goodly Heritage

Our church services were held in the home of Benuel and Anna Blank yesterday, with five young people being baptized by our bishop, Christ Esh. A truly moving experience, to be able to witness this serious ritual. It renews our vows and our faith immensely to be able to grasp anew what the Lord Jesus has done for all who repent.

And you just can't write on paper the feeling of thankfulness for a rock-solid foundation and a priceless heritage we as plain people can have. But how often do I abuse this or forget? My dearest wish for our children is that they may follow this path. It makes babies and everyday cares seem so worthwhile, to raise them according to our faith in Christ.

[SEPTEMBER 21, 1992

Thank You

Thank you to everyone who wrote and sent cards since my letter about the quilt. I do confess, though, I felt so guilty, as I certainly did not mean to draw attention to myself or make anyone feel obligated to send a card. I was simply stating my feelings, but perhaps I am more a selfish person than I realize and it comes out in my writing. Anyway, thank you for the cards. I much appreciated them and it just made me smile—all this attention I was getting.

I suppose life is just that way for all of us. We have circumstances that give us the blues, but we can always laugh at ourselves and our *dumb gamach!* It's much easier to lay down your pride and admit it if you failed, although why is the hardest person to do this to your very own husband?

I guess because Gid is right about 95% of the time. Husbands are always so right, in the advice they give, and somehow I bumble along and think, *He doesn't know anyhow,* but sure enough, he was right.

[SEPTEMBER 21, 1992]

Chips in Church?

Like yesterday, before we went to church, Andy asked to take some chips and leave them on the buggy, because he gets these headaches if he gets too hungry. I told him he can and Gid said he shouldn't, probably he won't even eat them, he'll give them all to his friends. But as these things go, I said he'll eat them, especially with baptismal services, he'll get too hungry.

Well, last evening Gid said Andy invited his cousins and friends and they were all sharing and "I told you so." I gulped and acknowledged the fact that maybe he'll just have to suffer his headaches.

What do other mothers do with boys who get headaches? He eats a good breakfast of eggs, toast, and oatmeal, but it's just too long a span I suppose. Last evening after our company left, he came down the stairs and his face was so white, he was almost crying and said he's going to bed as his head hurts so bad. And of course, a mother's heart is like jelly sometimes.

Gid said if it gets too bad, he'll just have to go out halfway through services and eat a sandwich or a banana or something.

[SEPTEMBER 21, 1992]

A Good, Submissive Wife

My lines are full of laundry and there's an east wind and it keeps getting darker, so I suppose my wash is in for a good rinsing. I need good sturdy lines in the basement, but so far Gid hasn't provided any. And I just haven't nagged enough yet, or wheedled or whined or begged or cajoled or whatever it is that a good, submissive wife is supposed to do when she'd like to have something done.

[SEPTEMBER 21, 1992]

Andy!!

After reading last week's obituary of the husband who died suddenly, my heart was just broken for this mother and her children. Thank you for sharing your story, and I want to extend my deepest sympathy to you and yours. Also to the parents who lost their baby in Dry Run. It really makes you realize that each day is a gift of God and our lives depend on God's mercy.

The children and I were discussing all this after school today and Becky said very seriously, "What if I'd die?" and Andy told her, "That wouldn't matter."

Only after our horrified gasps did he

realize that it wasn't very nice. Becky is much like a mosquito to Andy.

[SEPTEMBER 21, 1992]

Dad Kauffman

Dad Kauffman is a patient at Chambersburg Hospital since Saturday evening. He was running a temperature and not feeling well that day. And by early Sunday morning he had difficulty breathing. So an ambulance was called, while Jr. and Jimmy fanned him to help him breathe till help arrived. The diagnosis was a bladder infection, which we believe he must have had for quite awhile, and because of his multiple sclerosis he could feel no pain in the bladder area. He was on oxygen and IV, but he seems to be gaining strength slowly now. I talked to him today, and he feels he's not improving as fast as he should, with his temperature being above normal. It will probably take awhile for him to regain his strength, as it seems a fever just takes his strength completely away.

Sunday evening all of us children went up to visit him, and it almost scared me how weak he was. But last evening we went up with Ben Lantzes and Grandma Kauffman and he seemed so much brighter. They're hoping they can bring him home tomorrow.

[OCTOBER 8, 1992]

Worse Than Dead Cats

Gid came home from work with a big, fat, black Labrador Retriever puppy. I think a few dead cats would have been more welcome in my opinion. At least we could bury them and they wouldn't be any bother. I was washing and Gid stuck his head in the door. "Aren't you going to look at my new dog?" I told him I could just feel myself giving up! I am not overly fond of dogs, although I've tried hard to put up with one puppy after another over the years for Gid and the children's sake. But the puppy is so great while he's cute and cuddly, then he gets long-legged and ugly, chews on porch rockers, chews up any shoes or socks, drags the wash off the line, chases cars, lies in my flower beds, and I feed him and no one likes him. But with a sigh I said, "Alright." This person gave him to Gid because he had a virus, causing him to lose the hair around his nose and mouth.

So far so good, but I'm tentatively holding my breath, as it seems too good to be true. He is actually very gentle mannered and quite lovable. We named him Duke and he seems to be intelligent...and I almost like him. He's the most homely-looking thing I've ever seen.

[OCTOBER 8, 1992]

Leisurely Seniors

Mom Byler and I went to Gettysburg to clean *Mommy* Byler's house on Wednesday. *Mommy* has a cozy house, filled with books and cards and old furniture. I love old furniture and she has a few pieces that must be worth a lot. I can't wait till I'm an old *mommy*. I'll just sit around and play Scrabble and eat popcorn with Gid. That will be the day, *gel Mommy*?

We never know from one day to the next what the Lord has in store for us, and I may never be an old *mommy*, but I think it would be fun. You wouldn't have to worry so much about your weight, 'cause *mommies* that weigh 200 pounds just look cute. When I'm with *Doddy* Bylers I think it's so cozy how *Doddy* pours water before meals and helps clean rugs and couch cushions. Probably when Gid is a *doddy*, he'll pour water for me and help in the garden too.

[OCTOBER 8, 1992]

Undependable Appliances

Housecleaning is now finished, so last week I decided to take my sewing machine in to Irwin Leininger to have it fixed and really enjoy my days at the sewing machine. I went with Irma Zimmerman on her weekly route to Lancaster and enjoyed my day with her.

Irwin fixed my machine and didn't charge anything. He's so funny. He said he doesn't want to become filthy rich, so he won't charge me. Anyway, I felt so happy on the way home, planning what I would sew with a few new pieces of material.

When we arrived home, I discovered my sewing machine was thrown over and broken for real!

I don't remember hardly ever feeling so terribly frustrated. It was actually no one's fault but my own. I should absolutely have put it in the box with Alvin sei Anna's machine. I got everyone a quick supper that evening, and tried so hard to be nice, but I snapped at everyone. While washing dishes I felt like slapping my dishcloth against the window, just to be rebellious, but figured I'd just have to go wash it later.

I guess I could have sat on the back porch with Duke and howled at the moon to vent my frustration. The next day our newly fixed refrigerator in the wash house gave out again—a week after having been in Lancaster. So with a sigh I called Irma and asked her to take both "lemons" along the following Wednesday.

[OCTOBER 19, 1992]

Puppy Woes

Last evening our neighbor asked to use Gid's spotlight (the kind you use to spot deer). They have skunks in their back yard. He brought it back, laying it on the porch, and Duke dragged it down on the concrete sidewalk and broke it. Oh dear, what next?

[OCTOBER 19, 1992]

Good Ol' Duke

Duke is actually the nicest puppy we've ever owned. He pulled the clothes off the clothesline and all I had to do was spank him a little and scold and he didn't touch it again. I like him a lot and can hardly believe it. He's the plainest-looking dog I've ever seen, but very intelligent and mild-mannered.

[OCTOBER 19, 1992]

Emily Update

Baby Emily is growing and doing well for us. She's two months old now and smiles and coos and is starting to play with her toys. Since she's becoming so responsive and playful, the girls are starting to pinch each other again. Even Andy enjoys holding her and fussing with her. She's very alert, but her little catnaps during the day are a challenge, although she's contented while she's awake.

. . . . .

Bedtime, and I will be glad to rest this evening. I was lengthening dresses today, and I feel grouchy and cross-eyed.

I also went on a diet. I must try and lose weight now. I have no willpower and look like a person with no willpower.

So between being hungry and my neck feeling like a coat hanger from lengthening dresses, I'm not in a good mood. I hate to lengthen dresses, and I wish I could have a whoopie pie and a glass of milk.

[OCTOBER 19, 1992]

Supper Chaos

Laura and Becky are washing dishes and I finished putting the icing on a nut cake for Jerry Zook's Mary's wedding tomorrow. I offered to make a cake for Dora, and I sure am grateful they mix up these cakes and no one knows who made them. It was in the oven while we ate supper and for some reason we had the most hilarious supper, resulting in an overbaked cake. Rosanne spilled a glass of water, Becky dropped a dish in the raspberry pudding, and Gid didn't know whether to scold or laugh. Finally our sense of humor took over and everyone was laughing, which had a couple of them running to the bathroom. Oh dear, I felt like such an absolute failure as a mother who runs a proper household. Amidst all this clamor, baby Emily was crying and needed her bath and bed. How did we ever manage before we had older girls to help?

[NOVEMBER 2, 1992]

To Socialize or Not to Socialize?

This Sunday we rushed home from church without eating dinner, as we had company from Sugarcreek, Ohio—Reuben Shrocks and Edwin Yoders and children. Reuben's wife, Katie, and I met at Niagara Falls three years ago and have been pen pals ever since. So we had a quick dinner of ham and cheese sandwiches, baked beans, macaroni salad, potato chips, etc., and let all the dishes set while we visited as fast as we could. I hardly got my dinner eaten, as I was so busy visiting! And it has to be serious if I don't eat much. I thoroughly enjoyed them, and Gid had never met the men, which he hadn't been too thrilled about, but it seemed they had plenty to talk about, too.

I always appreciate Gid's efforts when he tries to enjoy my sociable ways, and he's getting better. Then I try harder to give up to him when he simply does not want to go to weddings. We're invited to Aaron Lantz's Katie's wedding on Thursday, and I could tell he simply did not want to go. So after silently fighting a little with self-pity and all those other unhappy little darts which are not from the good Lord Jesus, I offered to keep Amos and Ruthie's girls for them. They will be corner waiters and will be gone for two days. Now I keep patting myself on the head and thinking I'm quite the nicest person there ever was, 'cause I'm happy and Gid is happy and Ruthie is happy.

And, Aaron and Priscilla, thank you so much for the invitation. I could hardly believe we were invited, and could hardly wait to go. But at least I can write in *Die Botschaft* what a nice person I am now!

[NOVEMBER 2, 1992]

Voracious Appetite

Duke, our big puppy, is growing fast and eating about as much as I imagine elephants do. I'm actually very fond of him, as he's the only puppy I ever met who has some sense. If we scold or spank him once for something, he will listen and not try it again.

Our gray cat was a nervous wreck the first few weeks and lived on top of the patio railing, but they have learned to exist together now.

. . . . . .

My diet lasted until I became too hungry. I just got too hungry, and decided to lose weight some other time when I'm not so hungry.

[NOVEMBER 2, 1992]

Buddies' Day

Wednesday we had buddies' day at Stephen Stoltzfuses. This was for the younger group I belong to and we never get too much accomplished besides our own hand sewing. We had around 18-20 little preschoolers and babies. So by the time coffee break and dinner were over, the day was soon gone.

The same day Mose Hostetler Sarah had buddies' day for the "old ladies" I belong to. That day is once every month and we usually work a lot. I could hardly believe what they accomplished that day. They knotted three comforts, quilted, sewed, etc., etc., and no one thought about it that I was missing except Aunt Sarah missed baby Emily.

[NOVEMBER 17, 1992]

That Quilt Again

I started a rose and green "Lancaster Rose" quilt this week. It is for a wedding gift for our friend, Bill Moon, who will be getting married on January 2.

Now the deer hunters are worried, because with a new wife for Bill, they can't live in Bill's house over the deer season. I'm secretly kind of tickled, wondering if they'll have to sleep in the shop or what!

It's kind of exciting to start appliquéing again, but, oh my, when I think of my basket quilt! It's so humiliating, my face turns red to think of it. The poor quilt is still on the loose, trying in vain to be sold. I think it is safe to say that I will never, as long as I live, make another black quilt with red and green baskets on it.

My friend, Lorna Yoder, thought perhaps the Herb Cottage might be a good place to display this quilt. So bright and early one Saturday morning we loaded all five of my girls, two of our neighbor girls, and Lorna's two girls in her old blue and white van, with the quilt in a garbage bag under the seat, and we bounced to the Herb Cottage.

Well, upon arrival, I started to feel smaller and smaller, as it looked a bit classy, and my opinion of that quilt was low. But we ventured forth, only to be greeted by a huge man inside the very classy room, smelling of exotic coffees, herbs, and teas. I don't remember what we said exactly, but it pretty much amounted to, "Why, I have a quilt. Do you want it?" He turned us down flat, and I would gladly have crept behind the dried flowers if I would have been able. But Lorna (who is entirely different from me) kept pressing her point and he agreed to try. He told us they supply 20,000 stores across the nation including Saks of Fifth Avenue in New York and he owns a farm in Vermont where they raise these herbs and he deals only in antique quilts of which he has 500. I felt exactly like the biggest dud and thoroughly wished I had never set foot inside the door. He reluctantly took the quilt, informing us that he'll put $450 on it, and I will receive $300. If he would have looked out the door and seen our old blue van with nine girls in it, he might have given me $400 and chalked it up to charity. Oh well, needless to say, his "clientele," as he called his customers, were not interested in things of such low degree. So Carol Duble, a local quilt dealer, asked for it and is now trying in vain to sell it. It's no wonder my face turns red every time I think of this quilt, and why do I subject myself to this embarrassment over and over? I could put buckles on it and use it as a horse blanket, I suppose, but then even the feed man and the vet would laugh.

[NOVEMBER 17, 1992]

Disposable Clothes?

What do you do with a little boy who is terribly hard on clothes? His school pants usually have holes in the knee by Christmas, his straw hats are all ripped and torn in a few weeks' time or else the horses eat it or the dog plays with it. Sneakers last only a few months at the longest, and finally you feel guilty for always scolding and threatening. Mom

Kauffman made him three new coats this year, one for Sunday, one for school, and a Tri-Blend denim for everyday. And wouldn't you know, the second time he wore the Sunday one, it had three holes torn right across the shoulders. I sighed and rolled my eyes and as kindly as possible managed, "Andy, what happened now?"

He looked really close and long and shook his head sadly and said, "Well, Mom, I don't know for sure, but it almost looks as if someone could have gone through a barb-wire fence with this coat on."

Now who do you suppose it was? Sometimes I feel like Tom Sawyer's grouchy old aunt he was always trying to evade, and I don't want it that way. How many spankings and scoldings are too many, and how much love should be balanced with this?

Gid is very good with Andy, and I am always thankful for this, and we must leave our concerns to the Lord, otherwise we just wouldn't make it.

[NOVEMBER 17, 1992]

You Said...Lice?!

Today I was in our schoolroom checking 35 heads for those dreadful lice. They had a most unwelcome discovery at Oak Grove, so we had a search at our school, too. I found nothing that resembled nits or lice, but I was not as thorough as the public health nurse was at Oak Grove.

My head gets itchy even to mention the horrible little creatures or whatever they are, but these things can happen to us all, I suppose.

[DECEMBER 1, 1992]

As Fun as Chocolate

Thank you, Katie Glick, for the helpful advice on weight control. Yes, I do agree, but as with other things, it's so easy to have all this information stored in your head and you heartily agree with weight loss articles, but to apply this to yourself and your eating habits is the ultimate test. But, quite happily, I am now losing and really feeling good about it. After two weeks of being consistent enough to refuse my ham and mayonnaise sandwiches and chips, doughnuts, etc., it's still coming off. I'm still trying to convince myself that lettuce and tomato and onion with mustard taste almost as good. In simple language, losing weight is not easy because you can't have what you want! No chocolate cake or pecan pie or all the food that is a delight to me. I have lost six pounds and it's almost as fun as eating chocolate. Not quite.

[DECEMBER 1, 1992]

"It Comes You Home"

Every grandmother enjoys giving their grandchildren candy, I'm sure. Well, my mother gave our children little boxes of candy called Nerds. These Nerds were the biggest nuisance, because they are tiny little chips and they spill them constantly and they roll under the furniture and melt. Finally, I told my dear mother, "No more Nerds." She smiled and listened to me, and actually for a long time our children had no Nerds.

The other week at Petersheim's there was a big red bag with "Willy Wonka" written across one corner and I thought it sounded familiar, but the big red bag of assorted candies went into my grocery cart, thinking this will really please the children. They all had some, and Laura sat on the porch swing with this little pink box swinging happily and said, "I just can't believe you bought this candy, Mom. It's like *Mommy* candy."

I looked and sure enough, it was NERDS! I rushed into the pantry and just like a bad dream, that red bag was filled with all kinds of rolly little balls and pellets and chips. On Friday, when I did my cleaning they rolled out from under rugs, behind the stove, under the couch. Everywhere I went these little candies came rolling, bouncing, and pinging away from my broom. There was one bag called "Dinosaur Eggs" and those things I actually had to run after and catch with my hands. Needless to say, whenever you talk about something, "it comes you home." Because I don't know how often I made the remark, "I will *never* give my grandchildren any Nerds." Seems I couldn't wait that long.

[DECEMBER 1, 1992]

Ouch! Poor Duke

Duke, the puppy, is growing and is retrieving anything the children throw, and drops it faithfully at their feet. We just love our dog, and the other morning they were practicing their batting before the driver came for school. Andy swung, missed the ball, and hit poor Duke squarely on the nose. What a yelping and howling erupted! I went charging out the door, only to be greeted by Andy, and his eyes looked like two pools of misery. Fighting back tears, and the girls watching in horror, poor Duke was petted and held and consoled and fussed over until he quit crying. Andy even gave him a reassuring pat just before he jumped into the school van. A few minutes later he was on the porch, eating his dog food, and he looked at me, and I declare he was laughing. He just looked as if he had learned how to create a bunch of attention. Dogs are really quite intelligent creatures, and I suppose that's how they earned the title of man's best friend.

[DECEMBER 1, 1992]

Letters and Coats

Thank you, Rebecca Ebersol, for the reminder to keep our letters short. Perhaps I'm making myself at home too well and stepping on people's toes with my fuss. And now I must make an excuse for not making coats. Did you ever try and make one left-handed? All the material gets stuffed between the machine and the needle! I'm very left-handed and thus not very talented on the sewing machine. So

I'll make quilts and let you make coats and we'll exist in Pennsylvania quite peacefully together.

[DECEMBER 14, 1992]

Gone Batty

John Esh sei Martha was feeding her baby in the middle of the night and heard this strange scratching. Thinking it was a mouse, she lit a candle, only to discover a bat! Upon being revealed, the bat promptly started to fly around the room in their haphazard fashion, causing Martha to make a dive under the covers with a piercing scream. Poor John was frightened out of a deep slumber and shot out the other side of the bed like a rocket, trying to catch this strange object. In the meantime, Martha peeped out to reassure John that she thinks bats are harmless, only to discover that he . her bonnet on, tied securely under his chin. I wish I could write it as Martha told me.

[DECEMBER 14, 1992]

Snow Fun

Our children are all coughing and fighting chest colds since they almost drowned themselves in this beautiful snow. Andy would dive headfirst in a pile of snow, and Duke would bite his pants' seat or pull on his coat. They all had a hilarious time.

[DECEMBER 14, 1992]

Another Row of Beans!

Persecuted Banties

Saturday morning I parted the bathroom curtains, my morning ritual of checking on the weather and the world in general, and spied Duke with what I supposed was a boot, shaking his head vigorously. I closed the curtain and proceeded to comb my hair when I heard the most pitiful squawk. Oh dear, he's got one of Andy's precious long-tailed banties, and I rushed to awake him. He tore open his window and yelled at Duke, but the pitiful sounds continued. Andy jumped down the stairs two at a time, wearing only pants, and slammed through the door. A few seconds later he was in for more clothes, acting quite furious to cover up his little boy tears. If there is anything more precious to Andy than Duke, it's his banties and pigeons. So after rescuing the beloved banty out from under the patio, he walked across the yard with the poor tired chicken tucked securely under his arm and Duke skulking along beside him, getting the most thorough scolding of his life.

Gid has spanked him hard for chasing the chickens, but Andy said he just can't seem to leave them alone.

[JANUARY 11, 1993]

Fat Ladies and Anna

Six-year-old Anna told me this week that when our school sale was in August, I was talking to someone and a big fat lady came and stood on her foot. She was too embarrassed to say anything and her foot was securely stuck under this lady's shoe! She said she was there for a long time before the lady realized she was standing on a bewildered little Amish girl's foot.

She also informed me in the same

conversation that she can't see why I think I'm so famous for losing ten pounds. "You look exactly like you always did," she said, with her head tilted to the side, eyeing me quite critically. As I said before, children keep us humble.

[JANUARY 11, 1993]

Weighty Matters

Laura is busy in the kitchen this evening, preparing tuna salad and Jell-O for her lunch tomorrow. Unfortunately, my girls seem to have inherited their mother's weight problem, and I try to encourage them to watch their weight. It's so provoking to Laura to watch her skinny friends eat five or six chocolate chip cookies and never gain an ounce.

[JANUARY 11, 1993]

All-Purpose Mom

I'm expecting Mom, Eva, and Ruthie to help quilt today. Put a roast in the oven, fix a salad, clean up the house, comb the girls' hair, feed Emily her fruit and cereal, etc., etc. How many of you mothers know exactly what I mean? And I try so hard to be cheerful and smile and be nice when the pressure's on, but I always holler at least once and too often Andy is the target. He goes out to check the depth of the puddle in the pasture, and comes in with a big brown stain on my freshly swept floor. When will I ever be a perfect person? Or I'd even settle for being a better mother.

[MARCH 9, 1993]

Murder!

Gid is in the goat business now. He's buying goats at the livestock auctions and putting them all in one big pen.

Unfortunately, Duke took a thorough dislike to these goats and killed one baby goat. We were all away for the day and weren't at home more than five minutes when Andy came to the back door and quietly said, "Come here, Mom." There was a little white goat on the patio with blood over everything, partly eaten. It was so shocking I almost couldn't stand it! The poor little goat! And Duke, our own dear dog. We just stood there, too shocked and scared to do anything. I told the children we'll just have to sell Duke. We just can't put up with him eating innocent domestic animals. When Gid got home he spanked Duke, then tied the dead goat to Duke's collar and tied him down in the barn. All the children were crying, and I was almost, I pitied him so bad.

Things were almost in an uproar for awhile. But he evidently learned the first time, because Gid bought a few more last evening and one little one wandered out of the pen and Duke left it alone. But Gid spent most of the morning out searching with a lantern thinking Duke killed another one. He found it, quite all right, and I was so relieved. Everyone says he's probably at his worst puppy stage, at eight months old, and we'll have a good dog yet if he's properly trained. I hope so; he sure has gotten into a lot of trouble already.

[MARCH 9, 1993]

Gone to the Auction

Gid took the five oldest children along to the livestock auction last evening, the first time for Anna and Rosanne. Their eyes were like little stars when they came home to tell me about the sheep and the goats. One even jumped out of the ring into the crowd of people. I was home pitying myself with baby Emily.

[MARCH 9, 1993]

Improved Looks?

Amos and Ruthie had a taffy pulling Friday evening, and Jimmy helped the pullers by showing them how to do it, but was unable to help of course. That evening Israel's Mose lit a match to light their propane light and there was "poof" and it exploded into his face. Evidently there was a leak somewhere in the valve below the cabinet. He is minus his eyebrows and eyelashes and has a few scars and swollen eyes, but the burns were minor. He sure looks funny, though, and it certainly didn't improve his looks. We wish him a healthy new crop of eyelashes and brows, *gel* Mose?

[MARCH 9, 1993]

Touching Songs

Elmer Fisher sei Lydia had two quiltings last week, and I was invited Thursday with the Kauffman aunts and cousins. They were all learning new songs, and I loved every minute of it. I was so glad my back was turned except to Ruthie and Eva, because those songs went straight for my heart, or eyes, whatever it is that causes you to cry. I often wish I wasn't so emotional, and feel ashamed when I get all goose-pimply and promptly get tears when someone sings so nice. Lydia's dinner was so delicious, and we had a break in the forenoon and one in the afternoon. Oh dear, what is a poor person supposed to do?

[APRIL 5, 1993]

A Forgiving Husband

Our trip to Michigan was greatly enjoyed, and we had no blizzards to detain us. We had lots of fog and some rainy weather, but all in all, we were glad we went.

At our one stop little Gideon Troyer made our day. He hid beneath his bed and stayed there until the vet came and his curiosity won over. Then he came out of hibernation and went to the barn. Verna said he almost always hides under the bed or the couch when company comes.

We arrived home Saturday evening at 11:00 P.M., tired but what a good feeling to come home again! I packed a duffel bag for each older child, and really liked that better than trying to stuff everything in one enormous suitcase. I remembered everything but Gid's T-shirts. *Oh dear,* I thought, *how stupid of me, and he looks as cold and unhappy as a wet rooster.* Nothing to do but announce loud and clear, "Uh-uh-uh, Gid, I forgot your T-shirts. I don't know how..." only to be interrupted by a loud snort and words to the effect of agreeing that it was extremely dense. All of a sudden the humor of it hit me so hard that I started to laugh helplessly, 'cause he was so cold and miserable. He shut the bathroom door rather soundly, and I sat on the bed and laughed until I was done.

He was a good sport about it though and borrowed one of Amos's. I'm sure Gid could have married at least ten girls who would have made him a better wife, and he does a good job of overlooking my stupidity.

[APRIL 5, 1993]

Ordained Leader

Our church services were held in the shop at Samuel Lantzes. Communion and lots of visiting ministers and bishops for the ordination. An inspiring day and a short one to sit and listen to the beloved story, the greatest ever told.

Israel Stoltzfus is our bishop now, and I'm sure prayers are appreciated and needed. His age is 39 and his wife is my sister Eva. They have ten children ranging in age from sixteen years to eight weeks old. I suppose they would feel their duties are numerous, but the love and support of all of us will do wonders.

[APRIL 22, 1993]

Planting Time

Our garden was plowed this year with great expertise! It looked so easy. The mules plodded round and round, and Dad Byler and Emanuel knew exactly what they were doing. It's absolutely amazing how simple and easy it looked. So this week Gid had the harrow and one mule and did a good job of getting ready to plant. We planted peas, onions, and radishes. It was still almost too wet, but it's so late this year, with all the plentiful rains.

[APRIL 22, 1993]

Fascinating Kids

The grass is so green and Dad has a herd of 22 goats in the pasture across the road. They are a mixture of brown, black, and white, and it's sure more fun to watch them than starlings hanging on the telephone wire. Those little baby goats can be standing still and in a second they explode with exuberant energy, jumping straight up and doing a little dance. Our herd of goats was turned out to pasture, with Duke whining and crying on his chain in the barn. We release him every evening, and he's one black bundle of joy, galloping across the yard and running with the children.

[APRIL 22, 1993]

Prayers, Please

As most Franklin Countians know, we're going through a difficult time right now. I could probaby fill a few pages of *Die Botschaft* with my *gafuss,* but it all amounts to unkind people doing unkind things to dumb people like us who didn't know any better. They say the darkest hour is just before the dawn, so with our faith in God, we'll travel on. Prayers are needed, and God bless you all.

[APRIL 22, 1993]

Blooming Beauties

Everywhere a person goes, the Lord's loving kindness is in full view. Trees are bursting forth with beautiful shades of green, and fields are a waving mass of rich color. Tulips, azaleas, and rhododendrons are breathtaking this year, and a soft gentle rain is refreshing everything this morning.

We also have the biggest and best crop of dandelions in Franklin County.

[MAY 4, 1993]

Boys Will Be Boys

Andy went to Israels for overnight on Friday and stayed for the day on Saturday. He was so excited, and evidently it was every bit as fun as he imagined.

He claimed he slept with a nail jagging his backside and the mattress had ants in it. They made their own eggs and pancakes for breakfast and they weren't very good.

This was in their little cabin. That doesn't sound as if Eva is much of a housekeeper! Anyway, they went fishing at the creek and caught seventeen salamanders and saw a snake three-and-one-half yards long, according to Andy. They fell into the creek, and unfortunately, had to go swimming, in April! Andy claimed it was so cold you couldn't stand it, and the current was so swift, whoever was wearing big knee boots stood in front so the current wasn't as strong. He was laughing so hard to tell us that he could barely talk, and Gid was actually wiping tears by the time he was done. I asked Eva on Sunday what she thinks of these boys, and she said she didn't hear anything. It's just normal everyday stuff for their family of eight boys.

[MAY 4, 1993]

Chewed-Up Rocker

Duke is still here, bigger and blacker than ever. We keep him tied during the day, but when Andy gets home in the evening, he is allowed to be free. One evening last week he chewed up my one wooden porch rocker. It has like a basket-woven seat, and he almost ate it. I was so furious, I believe I actually could have shot him. Those porch rockers were long-sought-after and finally-acquired objects for me, and he actually chewed one all apart. I fussed and fumed and told Andy that now this is it, we are not keeping this dog any longer. If we total up four goats and one wooden rocking chair, we've paid dearly for our free Labrador Retriever.

But my heart melted again the next time he looked at me, and here he still remains. I just can't figure it out, as I never liked dogs at all. They yap and jump on you and have hair all over the place and I never even liked them at all. Until Duke.

Now I can understand why people cry when their dogs are killed. Daniel Flaud sei Miriam was telling me how their Lassie was hit on the road and she was almost crying, and Sarah Flaud asked if I heard about Daniel's Lassie, all emotional. I tried so hard to have real sympathy, at least one tear, or something to show my feelings, but I just didn't understand back then.

Duke is gentle and very mannerly, he's quiet and lies down so calmly and looks at you with his funny yellow eyes. Very friendly and extremely gentle with Rosanne and even little nine-month-old Emily. But he's got a few big problems, and he's mischievous. Thank you to everyone who wrote with advice, although as you can see, he's here to stay.

[MAY 4, 1993]

Sold!...for $400

The fire tax meeting was held at Jakes on Saturday and the Amish school sale was there a week ago. They are probably ready to relax and take it easy for awhile.

The school sale was a success and everyone seemed pleased with the turnout. Especially me. My black quilt sold for $400, and I just smiled and smiled and "thought me smart" (in the Dutch language). Stephen Lee's barbecued chicken was absolutely the best. Also, the doughnuts were extra soft and simply delicious. I can get thrilled about good food, and that's an important item at school sales.

[MAY 17, 1993]

Bye-Bye, Duke

Duke is gone now. He chewed up my other porch rocker and tore out a small newly planted maple tree, and Gid decided this is enough now. So we called a dealer and he came to pick him up and of course I had to help load him into a tiny little kennel on the back of a pickup. Poor Duke, he whined and cried and begged to be free, and I felt absolutely awful. I started to cry like a baby and sobbed to Sue Kendig, a friend who was here. She looked at me totally unsympathetically and probably wondered if I was okay. So now that's the end of the Duke stories and all the readers will probably sigh with relief. I never want another dog. SOB!

[MAY 17, 1993]

Vanishing Hats

Andy lost his straw hat, and summer isn't even officially here yet. He was over at Doddy Kauffmans and the horses must have eaten it, because it vanished into thin air. So now hat number two has a ribbon on and looks brand new for about six weeks. Hat number three is patiently waiting on the closet shelf till it's his turn. I don't know what I'd do if I had five Andys.

[MAY 17, 1993]

Improved Slave Driver

This is a busy time of the year. Everyone is working outside and it seems so late or something. School is over now, and the children are happy to be home this year. I must be improving as far as being a slave driver and tomato soup maker. Our garden is huge this year, with seventeen long rows of Strike string beans we're raising to sell. The children and I hoe together and I love it. They don't. They sigh and complain, but after we're working together awhile, they enjoy it. They just don't know it yet.

[MAY 17, 1993]

...Maiden All Forlorn...

Thank you to all who wrote or sent cards about my "sob story" paragraph. I should have been more informative. It was financial in nature, but as so often occurs, there are two versions of our story. One is the truth and the other isn't, so we will just watch, as the truth always reveals itself. It hurts, though, and I almost felt like the maiden all forlorn who milked the cow with the crumpled horn. In almost every situation there is some h but I wryly admit, it sure hasn't been easy finding it. Oh well, in everything that happens in our lives, there is a purpose and a lesson to be learned. I'm on lesson 999 now, and am still learning. We keep improving, hopefully.

[MAY 17, 1993]

Taking Mom's Place

Amos and Ruthie are the happy parents of another little girl named Martha. Mary and Miriam were our little guests for a few days while Ruthie was in Juniata at Mollie's. Because of Dad being sick, Mom was unable to be there the first day, so I was the second-best substitute. I tried hard to act and do nice things like Mom usually does, but am sure it wasn't Mom to Ruthie. I suppose I'm just an oversized *bupp,* but I really enjoy Mom's care a day or so when I have a tiny baby, and thought Ruthie would kind of have to swallow a lot to do without Mom.

Little Martha is so adorable, with dark hair and long wide eyes in a little round face, just like an Eskimo baby.

Tomorrow I want to check up on them again, along with all of my girls. Israel's Anna is there this week to do the work.

[JUNE 1, 1993]

Amazing Discovery

Becky just made an amazing discovery in church two weeks ago. She discovered for the first time in her nine years where Jake Flauds live. She knew who they were, but she never knew where they came from Sunday mornings. She always thought Daniel Flauds lived there and that's all. She was so relieved to finally find this out, as she often wondered where they live and always forgot to ask me!

[JUNE 1, 1993]

Escaped Pigeons

Andy had a tremendous loss this week. Someone left the door of his pigeon house open and they all flew away except for five. He had raised some of them, and try as he might, the tears just flowed and he cried like a three-year-old. They were so precious to him. After cleaning the pens and talking this over, he decided to square his shoulders and start all over again.

Why does your children's pain hurt almost as much as your own? I sure hope I can cope better with big important things when my children are older. I can hardly stand it; I pity them so much. How would "it go me" if they ever got hurt really badly or other things you can think of?

[JUNE 1, 1993]

Patience, Please

Poor Emily has something like cold sores on the inside of her mouth. The doctor says it's the herpes virus and they became infected. Needless to say, she is very miserable. She eats hardly anything and takes only short naps, crying a lot when she's awake. Oh, for more patience!

. . . . .

Laura told Rosanne to tear off the calendar page, meaning only May. Rosanne proudly marched over to the chair and ripped off every single sheet in one try, leaving Laura doubled over with laughter. Rosanne is three with very limited vocabulary, and she turned around and looked sternly at Laura and said, "That matters not; it looks cute!"

[JUNE 1, 1993]

Critter News

Andy is pounding away on his new pigeon pen this morning. Jr. gave him a pair of fancy pigeons, and his future looks extremely bright. His dearest wish is to own a pair of peacocks someday, and I keep telling him they're noisy creatures. In his small world, the more noise they produce the better they are. But I'm being very careful of any small critters on this farm since Duke.

. . . . .

Some of the goats slipped through the board fence yesterday while we were in church and ate off all the bottom leaves of our small oak trees. They also ate the new grape stalks. And last week, I noticed green flies in the windows of my wash house, and finally smelled something really yuck. I told

Andy to look under the patio; something smells really bad. Directly under the back door was a dead cat. Very dead! In fact, dead for awhile. Gid told Andy to crawl in and get it, which he did without too much pleasure and produced a black and white cat, or what was left of it. The girls stood around and gagged and said "gross" or "yuck" or "Andy!"

. . . . .

Chocolate the pony is severely lame this spring, much to the children's regret. She has a swollen knee and it keeps draining and seems to be getting worse. I sure hope we won't need to sell her, as the children drive her all over the place, and she is so lovable. It's nice to have a pony, but it would be better if all six of the children would fit on the cart as we always have this bargaining and "Mom, it's Rosanne's turn to stay here." Whereupon Rosanne bursts into the most heartbreaking howls, and two others try to console her, with promises of a piece of gum or a key chain. Then after it's all settled who will go along comes the enormous undertaking of catching this fat, spoiled little Chocolate.

"Do we have any carrots? Do we have apples or candy or just about anything?" Armed with all this ammunition, they venture forth, only to have Charlie, the driving horse, with Chocolate on his heels, lift his tail and gallop away. Success means catching Charlie first, then there's more hope of luring Chocolate with a treat. Usually, their faces are red and they're sweating, and Andy and Laura have at least one major explosion, leaving Andy marching stiffly to the barn, muttering under his breath and shaking his head at the unbelievable stupidity of his sisters.

[JUNE 14, 1993]

Dreaded Beans

Our seventeen rows of string beans are flourishing under the warm sun. The children eye them with absolute dread, and sigh and shake their heads.

Andy said he wishes all the goats would get out and eat every single bean stalk. We have never raised anything to sell, and I don't know what kind of produce farmers we'll be. The future looks bleak, as I can imagine Andy siccing the goats on the beans, and all the girls going to the bathroom or getting a drink and me picking beans!

[JUNE 14, 1993]

Diet Begone

I'm not doing too great on my diet anymore. I have serious reasons for not losing any more weight. My clothes were getting too loose and I dislike sewing. My dentures started to feel loose, so I imagined I'm losing weight on my gums and I really can't afford new dentures right now. My main reason was things like pizza and chocolate shoofly. I missed them so much.

[JUNE 14, 1993]

Oh, Those Beans!

Our beans are ready. After washing and ironing, we hoed and pulled weeds in our huge garden. After lunch I told the children, "The time has come." It was very warm, but we all got five-gallon buckets and ventured forth, bent our backs, and proceeded to pick beans. It was fun for about 15 minutes. Then the sun beat down harder and my back started to hurt.

Laura sat down in a row and Andy sat on his bucket. Becky went into the house for a pitcher of ice water. I kept on going and steadily feeling worse. Becky brought me a large glass of water, and I set it under a pumpkin bush and kept going. Finally, I was in so much pain, I didn't know if I was going to survive this ordeal or not. So I sat down and squashed a bean stalk, and I was too miserable to care. I was thinking the most depressing thoughts and pitying myself immensely. "How could we be so dumb, planting all those beans?" Never again, as long as I live, will I try and raise anything to sell—not even one little radish.

Eventually, though, a big beautiful breeze came along, and the relentless sun hid behind a cloud. The children starting stealing each other's beans, and throwing them at each other, and making up silly bean songs, and I smiled a little.

Just when I was wishing Gid would come home from work and see me out there acting so strong, a thunderstorm came up and chased us out of the bean patch. So now eleven more long rows remain for Wednesday, and hopefully we'll be better produce farmers on Wednesday. We probably picked five or six bushels, and we have many more out there. Oh, groan!

[JUNE 28, 1993]

By the Pound

Buddies' day was here on Wednesday. I had a "Lancaster Rose" quilt in frame, and we missed Levi sei Becca, Bennie sei Barbie, and Dora Zook. Ben Lantz sei Bena was here, too, which was special, as she dropped out a few years ago. We all weighed ourselves on my digital scales. Now in three weeks Elmer sei Lydia will have it, then we'll weigh ourselves again. What fun! I better say good-bye to my pizza again.

Tuesday the Kauffman aunts and cousins were to the Belleville area, where Aunt Fannie Peachey had a quilting for us. I thoroughly enjoyed the day. She had the most delicious dinner and vanilla pie that was perfect. Oh, I love vanilla pie and a scoop of vanilla ice cream to go with it!

I left Emily at home with Laura, feeling guilty and not very motherly, and as is usually the case, she was so good for the girls, and I didn't need to worry.

[JUNE 28, 1993]

Foot in Wheel

Andy caught his foot in the pony cart wheel and really has a bad wound. All week we've fought the infection, and I believe we have it licked.

It was a large area just "sanded down" through his shoe and sock and into the flesh.

[JUNE 28, 1993]

Glad to Be Alive

A cool breeze is stirring the trees and the creek is tumbling over rocks, and I'm sitting here at Enos Zimmerman's picnic grounds. The children are splashing in the creek, and Emily is sitting here on a blanket playing with her toys.

Lots of heat and high humidity is accompanied by thunderstorms almost every evening. Rain was like a miracle sent from heaven and it refreshed everything, changing the landscape into a lush green again. Gid said the farmers are really smiling, and I can well believe three inches of rain would make you feel like smiling. God is good.

[JULY 12, 1993]

Welcome Visitors

On Wednesday *Doddy* Sam Z. Bylers and Levi Stoltzfus sei Martha and six children surprised me by coming for the day. What a pleasant surprise it was! Mom Kauffman, Ruthie, and Israel's Anna were also here to help pick string beans. Poor Grandma, though, came to help me with my quilt, and it was all done. She was disappointed and no wonder, as she enjoys quilting. And then she ended up in that bean patch, happily picking bucket after bucket of beans. The girls were fascinated and Ruthie said she was very entertaining.

Doddys brought two buckets of sour cherries which was turned into pie filling. The day was just too short, as I always treasure the time with *Doddy* Bylers. I always tell the children we're lucky to have them.

[JULY 12, 1993]

Ambitious Aspirations

The bean harvest is over after only one picking because of blight. The three inches of rain caused it, I'm guessing. So we pulled out all the bean stalks and threw them over the fence to the goats. We haven't acquired a great wealth with thirteen bushels of string beans, but we live and learn.

Next year I'd like to have my own little produce stand and bake some goodies and have a few crafts and all these ideas swimming around in my head. A perfect garden with no weeds, and sweet children that willingly stay at work. Laura baking in the kitchen. Andy picking something. Becky and Anna picking something else. Emily perfectly good and clean. Who knows, could be the next Shady Maple? The real picture is probably more normal—the sun is unbearably hot, the beans blight, the whoopie pies flop, Emily cries, and my back is permanently bent. Seriously, Gid says the work is good for the children, and I did notice it helps them to be more content and relaxed after a forenoon in the garden.

[JULY 12, 1993]

Delightful Mollie

Last week I was invited to Maryland to Sollie Kurtzes to a quilting. Sorry, Mary, that I wasn't able to come. Gid thought I should stay at home, as we had two extra children last week. Little Mollie Van Lieu, who is seven, stayed with us for a week, as her mother had an operation. And I keep Keith Appleby who is five.

Mollie is a delightful child. There's just no other way to describe her. Perfectly straight thick blond hair and her front teeth missing and the most winsome sense of humor. She won all our hearts, and Becky almost cried when she left. Keith is an easy child to keep too, and is so very polite and respectful.

[JULY 12, 1993]

An Unknown Favor

We had a surprise van load of Rohrers and Beerys from Virginia last week. They just did us a terrific favor unknowingly. We had the charcoal going to barbecue chicken for the neighborhood picnic, and they visited with Gid, keeping him from putting the chicken on till the charcoal was white—a long-standing argument between Gid and me. The result was perfect chicken, absolutely delicious, and we'll give the credit to the Virginians!

Thank you so much for coming. It was nice to meet you, and I can still remember your friendly smiles.

[JULY 12, 1993]

Restless Lil'un

Sometimes with Emily it seems like I hardly have a chance to sit and absorb and appreciate a sermon anymore. She is not a contented baby and church is not her favorite place to be. So it's either sit there and struggle with her or just go away and try over and over to get her to sleep. She has this dislike of sitting anywhere for a long period of time, and pushes herself out and away from me continually, till my patience wears thin and I smack her, resulting in a wail of disapproval and heads turn, and I'm given a few understanding smiles and probably lots of people think, *Oh, it's Emily again.* I suppose I was just too self-satisfied with Rosanne, who sat contentedly anywhere, while I watched other mothers struggle with their babies, thinking I was perhaps a better mother.

[JULY 23, 1993]

Counting the Grams

Friday afternoon we traveled to Ohio where we spent the night at Fred Hershbergers and attended the reunion, or homecoming as they say in Ohio, at Paul Millers on Saturday. Jimmys and Amos Blanks went with us, and Israels and Dads went with another load.

As these things go, the time was just too short together, and I tried to soak in every minute to the fullest. We had a wonderful time, catching up on news with cousins and eating a delicious Ohio-cooked dinner. I looked over my tray filled with ham, filling, scalloped potatoes, salads, Swiss cheese, and all the other goodies and thought, *Oh my, the grams of fat in here!* But it was quickly brushed aside and I dug in ever so happily.

I'm still trying to lose, and I find it rather amazing since I watch my fat grams. I eat a lot, only try and eat differently. My life looks a lot brighter since Miracle Whip has a fat-free product and Ultra-Light Promise margarine is very good with little or no fat grams.

[JULY 23, 1993]

Chicken Little

We have a Kauffman reunion on Saturday at Aaron Lantzes in Lebanon, and on Tuesday a get-together at Cherry Lane School in Lebanon, where Susie (Lapp) Riehl used to be our teacher when Eva and I were fat little first graders.

Oh, I'm sure it will be interesting, and Eva and I no doubt will have a few giggles remembering.

Every time the class would sing the hymn "When the Stars Begin to Fall," I would start to cry, and Eva would have to take me out to the privy and try and comfort me. I was always afraid the end of the world would come and I couldn't get home to Mom quick enough. I guess I was a bit like Chicken Little, running around with the sky crashing on my head.

Anyway, I'm looking forward to it, to show my children where I went to school.

[JULY 23, 1993]

Learning Submission

Gid isn't much for reunions, and we've come to a peaceful conclusion if he's happier elsewhere, then I'm happier too. If he wants to go, I'm always glad, but if not, the girls and I go and enjoy ourselves. No two people are alike, and in that respect, Gid and I are exactly opposite.

And it's a very wise thing to learn; you can't change your husband, so you change yourself to suit, right? It almost scares me how easily I can stay home an entire Sunday and enjoy it. I was always chomping at the bit, but since we've lived together for almost fifteen years, he grins and says he trained me almost right. I would say he's had quite a job, 'cause I remember when we were newly married how I thought this was going to be now. God surely knows what He does, and His ways are so mysterious and above our own, that we may as well just give up and let the Good Man go ahead and trust Him every day.

[JULY 23, 1993]

A Good Healthy Time

Elmer sei Lydia had buddies' day and we all weighed ourselves again. A few groans and some "happy notes" and fresh fruit for coffee break, and doughnuts. It was up to each poor fat individual, the good or the bad! We quilted on the girls' pillow shams, and I picked her cucumbers for myself. She has the biggest cucumber stalks, just loaded with them, and said they still have a lot from last year.

So I made bread and butter, banana, and lime pickles. I love to make pickles, and even if the children groaned to see me come home with all the cucumbers we had fun doing them. Even Andy enjoyed turning the Salad Master and peeling onions till the tears streamed down his face.

[JULY 23, 1993]

What a Day!

I am in a hurry, and have absolutely nothing to write because I'm too busy. I'm either coming or going these days, and mostly going. It isn't right. It just can't be *chite* if you don't even have time to stop and smell the roses. I don't have any roses to smell, but there are other relaxing things I don't have time for. School clothes to finish, a quilt in frame, corn, peaches and apples to do, going away, school sale coming up—it's absolutely hilarious. No time to even watch fat grams!

Becky thought yesterday it would be much better if she had just stayed in bed all day. She knocked brown sugar all over the kitchen and dropped the whole bowl of cookie dough on the floor. She spilled sugar in the pantry and spilled milk on the floor.

She got a very sore throat and fever by evening, then at 9:30 she accidentally knocked Emily on the floor, hitting her mouth, and it bled and bled. Poor Becky, wonder how today will go.

[AUGUST 12, 1993]

Of Peaches and Head Colds

An Amish peddler named John King brought me Loring peaches, and they were very nice at $8 a bushel. He sold me an extra bushel, assuring me my family is growing. Now is that good salesmanship or what? I also got two bushels of pears and they're waiting to be done in a few more days.

I hope my head cold clears up by then. I had the most miserable time doing my peaches, with both hands sticky and my nose running. My eyes watered and my head felt like it could explode.

I was sitting in my puddle of misery, thinking how really tough I feel when here come Bill Moon and Nancy from Bedford with his brother and family from New Jersey. I got up and tried to look and act presentable, but I'm sure they pitied me, sneezing and blowing my nose and blinking my little bleary eyes at them.

[AUGUST 23, 1993]

Loving Family

It is hard to believe that school is starting in five days. I dread seeing the children go back to school. I miss them so much and all is too quiet and dull. Even Andy is growing up somewhat, and we've had an uneventful summer as far as Andy goes. His pigeons keep him busy a lot, and he's always cleaning pens or making new ones.

Even Emily has straightened out her life since she started walking. She's so tiny and doesn't weigh quite eighteen pounds, but at least she's happy now. She never crawled, just sat in the middle of the floor and screamed. The girls held her a lot, but she tried all our nerves to a frazzle. But each child is different and born with a different temperament, and that's what we have to shape and mold while their precious little hearts are soft. Do we actually love our children enough? How often I long for more love and patience, and oh, for once and for all, to be a better mother.

How often do I lay my work aside and hug and cuddle them? Not very often, and it's necessary to take this time out when they're small to let them know how much we love them. They're so small and so trusting and so soft and make so very many mistakes.

They pinch each other and spill iced tea all over the floor and there are always pretzels and Cheerios under the table. They ride their scooters into Grandma Byler's shrubs and they full well know better. Andy tells poor trembling Anna exactly what he thinks of her losing his hammer, and Laura complains about baking another chocolate cake. Becky is pouting because I made her clean her room the second time, since it wasn't done right, and they all do so many wrong things at times. But do we still love our children unconditionally?

Yes, we do. The precious times when Andy needs a hug and a thank-you for helping me, when the girls grin and sing and play their harmonicas, when the little girls sit on the table patiently stabbing peaches with a fork and putting them in jars.

Yes, indeed, marriage and children are ordained of God, and love is the answer to making a house a real home. No, our home is not always a cozy picture. If you ever wonder how it honestly is, just come visit us and see! Everyone is noisy and the doors bang and flies drone around. The children chase each other, and Gid and I are probably having a heated discussion above it all.

[AUGUST 23, 1993]

Unwilling Workers

Becky is mowing lawn, and Andy and Laura are furious. Upon arriving home from school, they were so tickled that all the cleaning and baking was done and planned their project in the shop. When Becky wanted to mow lawn, I decided we'll just do it all this evening, which didn't suit the other two. Andy stalked out and slammed the kitchen door a bit harder than necessary. Whereupon I hauled him back in by his shirt collar and proceeded to lecture him on door slamming. He managed a grin and an, "Oh, is that how it is?" They claim it will clear off tomorrow, but it may not. Besides, I have a big wash for tomorrow, and a bowl of macaroni salad to make for Mom Kauffman, who is having the young people for a chicken barbecue on Sunday evening.

[SEPTEMBER 17, 1993]

Encouragement for the Staff

I just finished reading an interesting letter from John Karr, one of the typesetters for *Die Botschaft.* She and I are regular pen pals and I feel as if I had already met her through her letters. I really feel sorry for the staff at *Die Botschaft* because of the unkindness they receive from us plain people. All of us are only capable of doing as well as we can and we all make mistakes. Why don't we send encouragement and a kind word?

[SEPTEMBER 17, 1993]

Missing Arm

Jimmy lost his arm. Whoever heard of it? But the other morning he could not find his artificial limb anywhere. They all searched high and low with the results being that Jimmy had to give up and go to the pallet shop without it. He is on the nailer again, but it's impossible without the aid of the arm. At lunch little three-year-old Leroy looked at Jimmy and said, "Shall I go look for your arm?" And straightway, he marched upstairs and produced the long-sought-after arm, which he had hidden under a bed.

[SEPTEMBER 17, 1993]

Edible Insects

This afternoon I did the most horrible thing. I don't know if I'll be able to eat supper this evening. Mom, Ruthie, and I were shopping, and I was watching the babies while they bought groceries at Cresslers. The sliding door of Evelyn Crider's van was open and the yellow jackets were just provoking. I killed one with the flyswatter and he fell into my purse, so I fished him out.

After a while I looked at my finger and thought I had a piece of melted chocolate on it, so, ever enthused at the possibility of a tiny taste of chocolate, I licked it off. It felt funny, like a feather or something, and had absolutely no taste. I picked it off and examined this object and it was a yellow jacket leg! The big black behind leg!

Evelyn and Lester both were looking straight ahead, and I shook it off like the plague, and swallowed, and I could feel my face turn the brightest red. I just looked out the window, and was really quiet for a long time, feeling as if I should either crawl under the seat or just act really quiet and sad or something. It was the most awful feeling. I didn't even tell Mom and Ruthie. They'll never find out till they read *Die Botschaft*. I don't think I'll ever be that desperate for chocolate again that I'll resort to yellow jacket legs!

[SEPTEMBER 17, 1993]

From Joan

(Note from J.K. — If I might take up a little space in your column, Linda, I wish to thank you for the encouragement in your September 29th letter to *Die Botschaft*. Kind words are always appreciated. Being on vacation the week that letter was set for print, it took a week for me to catch up on the news, and upon checking your column out, I want to say to your readers everywhere—no, I haven't changed my name to John as printed, and want you readers to know that was not a mistake made by Linda. That was a typesetting error, which is regretted. Even though *Die Botschaft* is not for "English" eyes, it has enabled me to make some very valued pen pals and I always enjoy hearing from you all. Thank you, Joan.)

[OCTOBER 6, 1993]

Homeless Spiders

We're having perfect October weather with bright blue sunny skies, and crisp nights with everything bathed in moonlight. Housecleaning is a pleasure, with a strong west breeze to dry all the quilts, curtains, etc.

I suppose lots of spiders are losing their homes right now, with busy housewives cleaning everywhere.

[OCTOBER 6, 1993]

Battle of the Bulge

Laura and I have just returned from our two-mile walk, pushing Rosanne and Emily in the stroller. After a day of housecleaning and not eating very much, I should see some changes in my weight again. This battle of the bulge is not always funny. Sometimes I just feel like forgetting about it. We really enjoy our walks though, and it's good for our relationship, sharing things we otherwise might not share.

[OCTOBER 6, 1993]

Coals of Fire

The next time someone is irked with me, I'm planning on sending them flowers. Dads were away for awhile and Mom asked if I would do their yard, because they were planning on having the young people Sunday.

Well, it was raining Saturday morning, cold and wet, and my heart was not very charitable when the girls and I went to perform our miserable duty. Of course, Mom was so grateful and profusely thanked us, and I was too guilty not to tell her I wasn't very loving in the rain, mowing yard. Israel's Anna was running the weed eater and it didn't take long at all. I was having all kinds of unkind thoughts while trimming. The following week Beedles florist truck came with a planter made up of different houseplants, and I was so delighted and set it right beside the couch for us all to enjoy. The card said, "Thank you for doing the lawn, Dad, Mom, and Jr." Well, the longer that planter sat there the worse I felt. The Bible says if we're kind to our enemies it's like heaping coals of fire on their heads. My head was very hot, and I wished I could go over and mow Mom's lawn 100 times.

[OCTOBER 6, 1993]

Rosanne's "Hashlight"

Rosanne's dearest wish for awhile has been a little flashlight to tuck under her pillow at night, like Laura has. It was so touching, how she begged for a "hashlight." She says lots of words with an "h" because of her speech, and this "hashlight" was so very important to her. So I bought one at Wal-Mart and she bounced up and down and squealed and clapped her hands when I gave it to her. Sadly, a few minutes later, she was in tears because she couldn't turn the thingamajig to turn it on. There was nothing to do but just watch her joy turn to disappointment. A few hours later Gid came home from work with a little "hashlight" for Rosanne! And she could easily flick the button to turn it on. I think I liked Gid every bit as well as Rosanne did, right at that moment.

[OCTOBER 6, 1993]

From Bad to Worse

Church services were held here at our house on Sunday. God's word was brought by Ben Lantz and Israel. Ike Eshes and son Jr. attended from north *dale*, and three girls from Lebanon came with Priscilla Fisher.

I can't remember ever preparing for church services that rain poured steadily from leaden skies like that. That was good, and I sure didn't feel like complaining at all, because we Franklin Countians know better! But, oh my, all the other irking little misfortunes on Saturday. First, our water pump was not working, only air and strange black particles flew out of the faucet, and my refrigerator in the wash house breathed its last sigh and refused to cool anything. And we depend on our second refrigerator a lot, especially over church. "Oh, help!" I thought. Surely nothing else will go wrong yet. We were baking *snitz* pies, when I looked up and Charlie, the driving horse, with Chocolate, the pony, went sailing past the kitchen window, kicking up the turf of my manicured, mulched, and trimmed lawn! I think I would have sat down and cried long and loud if the two moms and Ruthie wouldn't have been here. And those horses were really out for a fling, 'cause there was no catching them. They disappeared over the horizon and Gid stalked after them, but soon returned and said they'll be back.

Gid was planning on hauling manure and plowing the garden, and the rain prevented him from doing anything. That was all right. I could accept it, I thought, till Becky dumped a great big bowl of potato peelings, etc. right smack at the edge of the soggy garden. So I slogged out and put the whole muddy mess into a bucket and threw it over the fence, and wished with all my heart the garden would look better. Oh well, I bet no one thought of it, and these things occur!

[NOVEMBER 3, 1993]

The Most Important

On Sunday Israel preached how someone asked whose calling is more important, the bishop or deacon's? The answer was "the young mothers with little children on their laps." "Oh, my," I thought, "how can I do better?" It was so humbling, and the truth of it hit so hard that I would have been most comfortable under the bench. As it was, I hung my head and squirmed quite uncomfortably. We need to pray for each other, and ask the Lord's guidance.

[NOVEMBER 3, 1993]

Growing Up

We couldn't attend Uncle Jacob's funeral in Ohio, and it was a disappointment. We had planned our Christmas dinner for the people who work for us, and we stayed home.

It was hard to do, and I actually felt like pouting or kicking the couch real hard, or something drastic.

But the next morning I had given up and didn't mind so much, and I think Gid was relieved. Isn't it awful how much "old ladies" can still act like spoiled children? I hate myself when I don't accept circumstances sweetly and patiently, smile kindly at Gid, and assure him profusely that it's perfectly okay. Instead, I have to get a mean lick in like, "Well, it never suits us to go anywhere with my family," knowing full well it was my own fault; I had picked the 10th for our dinner. Probably after I'm over the hill for real, I'll be all grown up and the most wonderful person.

[DECEMBER 13, 1993]

Birthday Surprises

Which brings us to the subject of my birthday! I didn't see the shower "old" Mrs. Joan Karr put in, but my mom told me. I felt so *cheap*, but it's just the most wonderful fun! The mailbox always has the best surprises, and I'm quite overwhelmed. So many unselfish, sweet people who write, and I'm not worthy of all this attention. I just love you all, and thank you, thank you, to all who wrote. I would love to answer personally to everyone, but I'll just keep writing for this paper. I got letters from ladies who were in their seventies, and yes, I agree, I am not old. It's just that when you see forty approaching and your children are growing up, you panic and run to the mirror and check for wrinkles and quickly weigh yourself, and it gives you the blues. But youth can be vanity, and our life is but a vapor and will all pass away.

That's when we seek the Lord's face, and a deep settling peace enfolds us, when we can realize these earthly things are temporal and we have another, more fulfilling joy awaiting us. His love and mercy is new every day, and we need to thank Him daily. How else would I ever have a chance?

[DECEMBER 13, 1993]

Morning Already?

Poor Anna! We overslept badly; with washing to be done, the house a mess, lunches to pack, and I'm flying around the corners, barking orders like the worst general. Quickly flipping Anna's bob up, and she sighs so resignedly from the fold of her chubby little arms, "Well, Mom, I guess I'll just have to eat my cereal with my coat and bonnet on." A first grader, and her worst nightmare is missing the school van.

[DECEMBER 13, 1993]

A New Sewing Machine

To Church...through the Snow

Now what should I write? Here I am trying to write a decent letter every week, and there's absolutely nothing to write about except our own affairs, and surely by now everyone is properly fed up with that. The most exciting things are the snowplow going past and watching the birds at the feeder.

Oh, I know what I can write about. Sunday morning was so much fun, getting good warm buggy blankets out, and tucking the children cozily into the buggy. The wheels squealed and screeched across the frozen snow, and our big black "Charlie-horse" pranced and danced along, feeling his oats, I'm sure. The roads were a solid sheet of ice, and there's a winding steep hill just before you get to Ben Lantzes. Well, I dreaded going down and tensed up accordingly, casting nervous glances at the steep incline across the road. Charlie started to slide, and so did the buggy wheels, as brakes were useless. I screeched at Gid to get over, off the middle of the road, and clutched poor Emily so tightly she could hardly breathe. Gid just smiled and we slipped and slid safely down the hill, and I bit my tongue hard, 'cause I'm always telling him how to drive and he doesn't like that very much.

[JANUARY 13, 1994]

Andy—a Reader?

I'm holding my breath, and almost afraid to write it, but I think Andy is starting to read books. Wouldn't that be wonderful? A quiet Andy and the girls peacefully playing or singing or doing other decent things. He actually enjoyed reading the book *Where the Red Fern Grows,* which he received for

Christmas, and claims he wants some more. He's never been a reader, and oh, how I longed for this. His *Doddy* Bylers gave him a little yellow kerosene lantern and he loves to do his pigeon chores with it. Every morning he lights it and goes down to the barn, as regular as if he had forty cows.

Israel's boys are getting a golden Labrador puppy, and he's excited along with them. But I can tell, it's a little hard to swallow.

Now he'll have to hear someone else bragging how wonderful their dog is. It's good to learn to be happy for others too.

[JANUARY 13, 1994]

Winter Blues

Twenty-one degrees below zero this morning with about two feet of snow on the ground! A real winter and God's majesty is evident every morning when the sun's beautiful rays touch the brilliant snow-washed world. It's exciting, but I'm not quite as thrilled as I was. I think perhaps I'm acting a lot like the children of Israel when they got tired of their manna from heaven. I'm tired of wet puddles on my kitchen floor, wet clothes drying on racks, wet scarfs, wet coats, soaked snow boots, and I'm sick of cooking three meals a day, and I feel like throwing my whole quilt frame out in the snow. In fact, I'd get a real satisfaction out of seeing that thing headfirst in a snowdrift. I have a bad dose of cabin fever, and I already feel better since I vented my frustration to all my *Botschaft* friends.

[JANUARY 19, 1994]

Stuck

Monday morning when I saw the school van go wallowing through the snow, and snow steadily pelting down, I had some misgivings. But seeing the snow came from the west, I thought it would soon stop. At eleven, Gid came home and they were stuck with a four-wheel-drive vehicle. He wasn't happy that the children had gone to school. So a bit later I called Enoses and their children were home and said Enos had been home for twenty minutes already. Oh dear, where were my children? Poor Anna, in first grade, so small and soft and chubby. Surely they weren't dropped off at Lurgan, a good mile of hills and twisting, turning dirt road! So Gid left on foot to look for them, and just as he left here they came. Such a cold bunch of tired children! Laura and Andy were tired, but in good shape. Poor Becky and Anna had no tights on, and the snow accumulated in fierce amounts over their snow boots, and their legs were little red chunks of ice. Anna caught sight of her mother, and burst into the most heartbroken sobs, and I simply cried with her.

Between gasps, hiccups, and sobs, she related the whole miserable adventure, and by the time she was done, I decided it was like conquering the North Pole for her. Oh, I know I'm a *bupp*, but they're only little once and they need lots of love and attention, don't they?

[JANUARY 19, 1994]

What's Next?

I miss not having buddies' day through the winter months, and I'm about ready for a real good argument again, and four or five chocolate chip cookies with coffee.

Dad Byler had his 61st birthday yesterday. We went over in the evening awhile, and had popcorn and gave him his cards. Everyone else was snowed in, I suppose. *Doddy* is special to the children, especially Andy. Seems they have a mutual interest in any living creature—goats, banties, pigeons, or whatever. And *Doddy* loves to play games, and it's nothing new to have them all whooping and hollering while they're at it.

. . . . .

Well, the time is here to get to my quilt again. Or I could bake something, or sew a white cape and apron for Becky. I don't feel like doing anything and I don't have a good book to read. It's too cold to go out, so I'll fix a cup of coffee and sit on my couch and pity myself awhile. Then I'll quilt again.

[JANUARY 19, 1994]

Injured Thumbs

I must hurry. Our school meeting and dinner is at 11:30, and I have a few jobs to do yet. I'm partially handicapped for awhile. I guess the Lord must have punished me for complaining yesterday about making a five-gallon bucket of potatoes. That was stretched, and not very nice. Anyway, while going full speed with my slicer, I sliced off about one half of my thumbnail, into the flesh. Ugh! It sure bled a lot already and I'm trying to be brave, but it hurts so badly. I wish Mom would come to exclaim over it and pity me. Monday I ran my quilting needle way up under my other thumbnail, and that hurt just awfully, too. So I better straighten up here, don't you think?

[JANUARY 26, 1994]

Elephant Look-Alike

On Saturday while doing the cleaning Andy kept sneaking into the pantry to eat potato chips. Finally, I lost my temper, and dragged him out, giving him a good scolding and a smack or two across the shoulders. In tears, he slunk into the living room and buried his sorrows in a magazine. So I went back to work, feeling guilty. I was on my hands and knees, scrubbing the kitchen floor. Awhile later, he sighed, got up, and walked past me, slanting me the most discriminating glance, saying, "Mom, you look like an elephant when you clean the floor." All right, I deserved that, Andy, and we had a good laugh together. I apologized for losing my temper, and he told me all his bottled-up frustrations of Saturday morning. It's not safe to be in the house, and oh, how terribly true. Sometimes our children are our best teachers, if we can humble ourselves enough. Eleven-year-old boys do not need an irate mother, taking out her Saturday morning dirty house frustrations on them. That certainly was not discipline, it was temper, and after all, he was shoveling snow and was really hungry for those chips.

[JANUARY 26, 1994]

Musical Cleanup Crew

Jolaine and Kara Zimmerman are here with the girls to spend the night, and I was treated to the most wonderful music while washing the supper dishes. Is there anything more beautiful than little children singing? All their innocence and youthful exuberance exploding into joyful songs of praise. Four little girls, and they all love to sing, and they clapped and stomped their feet.

[FEBRUARY 2, 1994]

Winter Wonderland

Saturday evening we joined Amos Blanks and Jimmys at Israels to remind Israel that he will be forty the next day. Cake and ice cream, and conversation, while the children discovered the wonders of these ice-covered hills. Laura fell, breaking her glasses, losing one lens, and scratching her nose, but that was all beside the point. They begged to stay longer, or just please let them stay overnight, as that story usually goes. But we piled the whole weary bunch in the buggy and fairly flew home, with Charlie thinking, *This is absurd, going away in the evening like this.*

[FEBRUARY 2, 1994]

Unsympathetic Sisters

No news, absolutely nothing else to write, and there is no use pretending I feel like writing, because I don't. I have a headache which is only normal because I won't wear my glasses. Mom Kauffman, Eva, and Ruthie regularly lecture me on the merits of wearing glasses, and they don't even pity me or offer me Tylenol anymore. I think it's awful how coldhearted they are getting toward me. No love at all, I claim. Well, no wonder, if I wear glasses I feel like a horse with his bridle on; I can't see out the side. And I can't kiss or hug my children right, or scratch my eyes. And when I cry I have a tremendous job. Take off the glasses, wipe eyes, wipe glasses, put them on again, decide they're not clean, take them off, wipe again, put them on, still not clean, repeat process all over again.

[FEBRUARY 2, 1994]

Forgiving the Goats

Oh, yes, our goats are having babies, every night there are more baby goats. Gid and Andy are so proud of them, but I'm still nursing a personal grudge because it's their fault we had to sell Duke. And they ate all my marigolds and grapevines last summer.

I'm working on forgiveness toward them.

[FEBRUARY 2, 1994]

Mom and Dad Kauffman

Dad Kauffman is receiving mail almost every day and is enjoying it, although I forgot to mention his name! Joan Karr sent them a card addressed to Mom and Dad Kauffman! His name is Mike S. Kauffman, and if you haven't sent a card, there's still time. He's been kept in the house almost all winter, and Mom says he does well for not more than he can do. He has a low window, where from his chair he can watch many different kinds of birds at the various feeders Mom has out.

Mom claims they're getting into a stale routine. Every morning when she washes the dishes, Dad will say, "Anna, the titmice are here." She'll say, "Really? Well, they're a little early, aren't they?" And Dad will say, "No, they're right on time this morning." And she'll resume her dish washing!

[FEBRUARY 9, 1994]

Oh, for a Bernina!

Lucy Zimmerman and Etta Hoover spent a day here, and I sure did enjoy my day. Lucy was crocheting an afghan, and Etta was cutting patterns. They both love to sew, have a Bernina sewing machine which they love, and claim it's no wonder I don't like to sew. Their advice is to get a Bernina and let your housework go, just sew and enjoy it! I don't have a very good machine. I bought it when I was seventeen and it has served me well all these years, but it's starting to show its temper. Lucy brought me a pile of books from her mother's, Mrs. Annie Gehman's, library and it's a fright. I hurry through my work and sit and read, read, read. I'm actually embarrassed to admit it. I never do that, just read like this.

[FEBRUARY 9, 1994]

Pulled - Apart Emily

Saturday evening we took Emily to the emergency room at the hospital. Andy had made the most exciting house on the couch with blankets and pillows, and he pulled her up into his house by one hand, resulting in quite a few tears and one arm hanging useless. By the next evening she was quite miserable, and the doctor told us it's not unusual. A ligament in the elbow had popped, and after some X-rays and quite a few attempts, he got it back in place.

Within five minutes she was her normal happy self, and I was feeling so grateful it wasn't worse. Needless to say, Andy felt extremely stupid, but it really wasn't his fault. Now we all know to never lift a child by the hands. The doctor told us to always lift above the elbows.

[FEBRUARY 16, 1994]

Just Like Mom

Israel's Anna is having a quilting for Laura and Becky tomorrow evening. She actually has a real wall hanging in frame, and the girls can hardly wait to go quilt and spend the night with Anna. Eva said they made cream-filled doughnuts, and the girls are already packing their duffel bags.

I noticed Andy sitting quietly and sadly on the couch tonight while I prepared supper. I'm sure he's indulging in an awfully big dose of self-pity, and I'm just waiting for the usual "Why do they always go and I never get to go?" So I'll try and have some sensible answer ready whenever the storm approaches, because I'm quite sure it's brewing.

[FEBRUARY 16, 1994]

First Time for Everything

Quilting is just the thing, but oh, for some exercise! These snowstorms and staying home quilting and picking at food have resulted in me gaining weight again. Sometimes it's discouraging, and you don't even care, and you console yourself with wearing glasses and getting gray hair. Youth is gone, so relax. There's a first time for everything and I never weighed 200 pounds yet!

[FEBRUARY 16, 1994]

Peaceful and Serene? I Don't Think So!

Two more snowstorms, and a bit of warm sunshine sandwiched between them. Cold winds are blowing this evening and the children are going sled riding by the light of the full moon.

Doesn't that sound peaceful and serene and like a picture book, with colorful children gliding peacefully down a gentle slope? Well, this is the actual situation.

The girls are washing, drying, and slamming dishes into cupboards as fast and furiously as possible. They persuaded Andy to sweep the kitchen in order to be finished quickly. And he is throwing afghans, kicking toys under the couch, and making five or six swipes across the floor, and every one of them is talking in various tones of voice, and none very quiet. The window above the kitchen sink is splattered with dishwater, the towels are slung haphazardly across the rack, but the sleds are waiting, and I remember the feeling so well.

[FEBRUARY 24, 1994]

Andy's Ideals

Emanuel and Rhoda are at Dads almost every day, working on the house, which they're planning to move into on March 9th.

There's a good bit of work to be done yet, and I want to help with the painting, etc. So they will be our new neighbors eventually. Andy is so impressed with Rhoda. Dad had two new baby goats, and Rhoda brought them in, dried them off, and was caring for them. Andy just couldn't get over this. He told me it would be "neat" to have a wife like Rhoda. I just smiled, knowing full well I fall short of his ideal of a loving mother to baby goats. I'm afraid I still haven't quite forgotten my personal grudge, but good things take time.

Andy has a new pony we bought from Allen Leids this week. He's big and I think he's beautiful. I love ponies. Andy goes down every evening and combs and brushes him. Now all we need is a saddle, bridle, harness, and cart. Oh, dear! Little lame Chocolate will remain. I could never bear to part with her. She is a pet to Becky, Anna, and Rosanne, and so tame and trustworthy.

[FEBRUARY 24, 1994]

Oh, for Some Spring!

Tantalizing patches of green grass are emerging from mountains of dirty snow. Killdeers and robins are appearing, in spite of the winter weather. This old-fashioned, exciting winter with its many snowstorms has lost all its appeal, and to be quite honest, I feel like sulking and not being a bit pleasant about the winter storm watch for tonight. But there's nothing we can do, and God is exactly in the same control He's always been, so I'll sweep up the dirty puddles, stack the wet boots by the stove for a hundredth time, hang the soaking wet gloves on the rack, sweep up the coal dust, and try and chirp a cheerful tune while I quilt. It will probably come out more like a snort or a growl.

[MARCH 8, 1994]

Honored Guests

Our church services were held at Sam Kings with sermons by our visiting ministers from Juniata County. Aden Troyer had the opening, John King of east *dale* read the scripture, and Felty Petersheim preached the main sermon. Menno Peacheys were also present from Juniata and Elam Fishers, Stevie Hostetlers, and Melvin Smokers attended from adjoining districts.

The Juniata visitors were here for supper, and we were so tickled. I never thought we would come near to their list of people to visit, but, sure enough, they were actually all here. Now all the ladies who have ever been to Mollie's (and have been served her delicious meals and received all that tender loving care), how do you suppose I felt? If you could weigh feelings, I would have weighed between 80 and 100 pounds! But in spite of feeling tiny, it was a time to cherish, and I am still as pleased as punch. My side of the family and Eli Dads were here too, and I told David Blank sei Mary they're welcome to come and was disappointed they didn't show up, as I know David would have enjoyed visiting with them.

[MARCH 8, 1994]

Acrobatic Antics

I laughed at Everett's wife Eva's wash hanging ordeal. Weren't we all simply acrobats at our wash lines this winter? You had your choice, stomp a hole through the crust and hurt your ankles, or go slipping and sliding, trying desperately to hang on to the clothes basket. But I'm not sure any of us could equal Jake and Sallie Flaud's stunt. They got out Miriam's bathtub, and I'm still trying to figure out what kind of bathtub, Sallie. Anyway, they both sat in it, and it wouldn't budge, so Jake got out and Sallie went flying down the hill in the bathtub, with David Alan running along beside her! So all this ice must have brought out the child in all of us, even *die mommies* and *doddies*. The smallest, bravest little person I've heard of was Levi King's Miriam, who is Emily's age. She sat in a little round saucer and went flying down the hill all by herself, and she's only eighteen months old.

[MARCH 8, 1994]

Sisters and Buddies

The girls have taken to dressing up in old caps and aprons, and take Tupperware containers with some sewing and have buddies' day, all in pretend, of course. Their conversation the other evening had my shoulders shaking silently at my quilt.

Seven-year-old Anna's husband was named Rudy, and she announced the fact that he's not very good looking, but he was so nice and friendly, she just had to marry him.

One of them had thirteen children, and they wished so much some of them would get married, but the girls ate a whole box of graham crackers before they went to bed, and they are so fat that no one wants them for their wife! Where did they think up this unbelievable story? But they were so sincere you almost felt sorry for them.

[MARCH 8, 1994]

Undesirable Attitudes

Yes, it's fun to have a family of six children, but somehow this week I was introduced to the helpless feeling of children harboring wrong opinions and attitudes.

Our oldest are thirteen and eleven, and somehow I've always had this saintly little halo over my head, thinking my children wouldn't ever be quite like some others, perhaps just a little better. Well, circumstances at school had Andy in a huff, and how can you pound different attitudes into one small, very determined little person's head? You can't. And for the first time you feel your own inadequacy, your simple helplessness, and it's very unnerving. Thank God for a sensible husband, who always gets me calmed down and straightens out my senseless fuss. Children are entitled to their own opinions, and the good Lord will teach them if we commit our children to Him. But oh, how my heart aches to realize the same bitter lessons I had to learn the hard way must also be taught to our beloved children. Isn't it all so humbling to really grasp the fact that we of ourselves are powerless? It's enough to drive you to your knees and beg the Lord to have mercy on them all; they're still so young and inexperienced. Sometimes my heart feels like a battered marshmallow. But I better straighten up and face life, 'cause I'm sure all you *doddies* and *mommies* realize I have much ahead of me. So let us pray for each other and for our precious little ones. May God bless and keep you all.

. . . . .

P.S. I'm sorry I missed writing last week, but the mailbox was buried in three feet of snow. I was partly sulking probably.

[MARCH 8, 1994]

A Real, Old-Fashioned Swoon

This is being written by my right hand very carefully. I am afflicted by a bad case of bursitis and have now given up and put my left arm in a sling. I will rest it for a week, while I try to be patient and remain as "fit to live with" as possible. I feel frustrated and grouchy and miserable. It's raining torrents of rain and the sky is gray.

This handwriting is awful. Laura must copy this. What would I do without her? She's quite a blessing, ironing aprons this evening. Saturday morning I was combing my hair and must have twisted my arm and pain shot down the whole length of my arm, resulting in me lying on the floor in a faint—a real, old-fashioned swoon.

Gid could not revive me or carry me, so he dragged me unceremoniously through the sewing room and stuck my head out the patio door.

Imagine! There I was, with poor Gid trying desperately to wake his conked-out wife. Well, it wasn't funny. I mean it. I was weak and sick all forenoon. And I've thought a lot about dying since. It's seriously not funny either. Gid really likes me now.

[MARCH 22, 1994]

Time to Stay at Home

Life is returning back to normal again, after having so much going lately. I enjoy going away, but not if it's persistently three or four days a week. Then I get grouchy and tired, especially if it's hot outside and you come home with things to be done and no ambition or energy to do them. It's really not fair to the children. Innocent little souls, they really can't determine their fate when Mom plans too much. And, most important, when Gid starts to roll his eyes and sigh, and I'm racing around here in an absolute dither, slamming soup on the table, it's time to stay at home.

[JUNE 28, 1994]

Major Project

After being bored for awhile, Andy has started a major project; he's building a real big pigeon shed, and I think he's doing a terrific job for an eleven-year-old. It has two windows, a door, shingle roof, and all. He's doing it all by himself, except asking Gid some advice. Today he made a frolic for Israel's Mike and Paul, and I'll have to send iced tea and cookies down for my "men." It sure makes a difference in life to have something to do.

[JUNE 28, 1994]

I Love My Bernina

I made five pairs of pants for Andy yesterday on my Bernina sewing machine. When I first started to sew, I was ready to throw it at Lucy Zimmerman, Etta Hoover, Miriam Flaud, and all the ladies who recommended them. And especially the Bernina man! I am very left-handed and this thing is very right-handed. I almost had to lie down to thread the needle. The foot has a crack to the right, and I was always used to pulling the thread to the left.

Nothing went right or felt right and I hated it! I felt like crying because we spent so much money on it. But I quit sewing, walked away, and read a magazine and pouted. The next day I sewed dresses for the girls, and everything went so smoothly, and I started to experiment with different stitches, and I perked up a little. Now, after sewing for awhile, I love my Bernina. I should have a sticker for our buggy, because I feel exactly like everyone else. I love my Bernina.

Laura pieced the "Dresden Plate" quilt and she likes it, too. So ladies, if you want a sewing machine that really works well, and is so easy to operate (after a while), try one! If Irvin Zimmerman of Hinkletown reads this, I'll send you a bill for advertising!

Also, the cabinet from Chris Sensenig of Ridge Road is another thing that was really worth the money, and I'm pleased.

[JUNE 28, 1994]

Tonsil Troubles

We had to take Rosanne to a specialist to check her tonsils. They're so big and swollen, and have been that way for close to a year. Our family doctor said she'll likely outgrow it. But I can hardly stand it, the way she breathes at night. There is an obstruction somewhere between the nose and throat because she breathes through her mouth, and you can hear her all over the house at night. But the specialist felt as long as she's resting well and not thrashing around in her sleep, we'll let it go for another year.

He said the decision is ours. We can watch her general health and when we're ready, he'll make arrangements as an outpatient to have them removed. Gid said last evening we might have to get a second opinion, because we had chicken for supper and she could hardly swallow the white meat. And she's so easygoing and patient, she never complains, except in the morning her throat hurts sometimes.

Anyone else out there have any advice? Years ago they removed tonsils more quickly than they do now, I think.

She's four years old, and the doctor said she already has an overbite from her swollen tonsils pushing her upper teeth forward. To be honest, I can hardly stand it, but am willing to do whatever he thinks best. I guess she'll be all right.

[JUNE 28, 1994]

Lessons from a Firefly

Fireflies are doing their best to brighten the dark world with their tiny lanterns. The darkest hollows is where they shine their best. Would to God that we too might shine with God's love where everything seems to be dark. One feeble little light can still illuminate a corner for someone.

. . . . .

I'm sorry to have missed the scribe gathering in Lancaster. My main reason was Gid not agreeing to go and we were in Chincoteague, Virginia, before that. We came home Friday evening with a load of hot, tired, sunburned children, mounds of laundry, and many other duties to attend to. I thought of all of you, wondering how it was, what you did, how you looked, and on and on.

[JULY 19, 1994]

I Hate to Quilt!

Monday morning Laura and I started to quilt the "Dresden Plate" quilt, and I may as well admit it, I hate to quilt when it's warm. Your needle sticks and your hands sweat, flies buzz around your head, and when you get the flyswatter they sit on your back till you put it away. As soon as you lay it down and peacefully resume your stitching, they gleefully fly past your nose and buzz in your ears. Hot air comes in the windows, the children whine 'cause there's nothing to do, and Emily discovers a bottle of Elmer's glue in the toy box. "I hate to quilt," I tell Laura and she calmly stares at me with no comment. Probably thinking, "Here we go again, the I hate to quilt routine." How can a thirteen-year-old daughter make me feel so immature? I looked at our reflection in the door and my hair stuck straight out, glasses sliding down my nose, cap askew, and she looked combed neatly and perfectly poised stitching away. Becky does pretty good for a small ten-year-old and I love the fact that the girls can help.

[JULY 19, 1994]

Sweet Corn

We had our first good meal of early white corn this evening. Corn along with fresh tomatoes and barbecued beef made a delicious supper. Our table is a disaster when we have corn on the cob. It looked so pretty before the family sat down. Neat dishes of butter, salt, and pretty red tomatoes sliced on a platter when, lo, the storm strikes. Chomp, chomp, chomp. "Pass the salt." "Where's the butter?" More chomping and passing salt and butter till the table looks very much like a tornado hit, not to mention the floor. Tonight I just stood and sighed, then resignedly got a bucket of warm water and scrubbed the floor around the table.

How do other families eat corn? There has to be a better, more delicate way. We don't eat corn in small quantities, either. More like five or six ears per person. Becky loudly announced tonight the most she ever ate was eleven ears—starting a healthly argument about how big the ears were, Andy declaring at the top of his lungs they were only tiny and Becky insisting they were ordinary big ears of corn.

[JULY 19, 1994]

New Occupation

Today I happened to think about school starting in five weeks and I forgot about the school sewing. I can't believe how dense I'm getting to be. Seriously, I have four scholars who will all need clothes and I never once thought about it. I panicked. When will I sew? It's going to keep me busy to finish this quilt and two wall hangings for our school sale. Laura said the week after the school sale we'll really sew fast and furiously since we each have a sewing machine. She's just learning, but every stitch helps.

. . . . .

I'm thinking of writing a book, since I hate to quilt so much. I would love to write a book, and I've started one several times. But I can't stand to read what I write! It sounds so dense and is worded all wrong, so I throw it away. If I ever do write a book my author's name will be strange. Then if people really like it, I'll tell you I wrote it. And if the book would be truly boring, no one would ever find out.

[JULY 19, 1994]

Getting Rid of the Tonsils

Rosanne's surgery went well on Friday. We had to get up at 4:30 in order to be in Carlisle at 6:00. Poor, tired Rosanne, sucking her thumb and hanging on to her doll, out into the cold night, the cold van, and away to her much dreaded surgery. The staff was kind, and Dr. Hershberger is a very good doctor.

Everything was normal routine for them, and was handled accordingly. Getting her to drink her juices was the most difficult part, as it hurt so badly, and she must drink. It's so nice to hear her sleep so quietly and comfortably now.

[DECEMBER 13, 1994]

Sweet 37

Today my sisters and mom came for coffee break, with ice cream and cake for my 37th! As my dear sister Mary signed her birthday card: "Sweet

37." They live 700 miles away in Michigan and are no longer members of our church. But, somehow, our hearts remain bound. She never fails to hit my chord of real humor, and our love for each other is precious, even after all we've been through. Who else could think of kind of sadly, yet humorously writing "Sweet 37"? We often think back and cherish our times together. Such is life, its mountains and valleys, and bittersweet memories, dark rainy nights of anguish, and always the night vanishes to a brand-new day. And what remains most real after all the trials and sorrows? Always the love we feel for each other. And even that, we can't really claim for our own, as it comes from the dear Lord Jesus.

[DECEMBER 13, 1994]

Otis

Andy got his puppy for Christmas a bit early. They found an ad in the paper with the price reduced on black Labs because they were nine weeks old. So Gid and Andy went to see them, and one excited Andy carried him in the door. He looks exactly like Duke, and they named him Otis after discussing names, or to be truthful, a real barrage of heated arguments. Tar-Baby, Napoleon, Thunder, King, etc., etc., etc. I really don't know when they decided on Otis, but Otis he is. He slept with Andy the first night, and was just fine. After that we decided he must stay outside, and he is adapting well. He sleeps in the barn with the other animals at night. Hopefully, he will be a companion for Andy for a long time. He takes him to check his muskrat traps and he loves the ice-cold pond water. (Otis, not Andy!)

[DECEMBER 13, 1994]

1995 That Otis!

All's Well That Ends Well

Israel and their little Linda and Dad Kauffmans had a mishap when coming home from church. Their horse shied and started backing, and they tumbled down a steep embankment, becoming entangled in a huge tree. It seemed like a miracle that no one was seriously hurt. Quite some feeling, to see how wrecked the buggy was, and find out they were all right. Dad had a few bruises, and Mom went to the emergency room, as she had difficulty taking a deep breath, also in turning her back. Only bruises and perhaps a cracked rib, as the doctor said they don't show up well.

But she's in pain, and spent last night on the recliner with her head on a pillow on the card table in front of her. She can't sit back against anything, so she spent a miserable night. Israel was not hurt, and we were all grateful, as it could have been worse. Everything has its reason, and perhaps our family needs Grandma's prayer vigil in her long nights awake. When sorrows and trials come upon us, and things seem so despairing, there's always hope, and faith that God is watching, and in His wondrous wisdom knows exactly the outcome.

[JANUARY 9, 1995]

A Boy and His Dog

The frigid weather brought the ice skates out of the attic, and I bundled up with the children to check out the neighboring pond—Andy, Laura, Becky, and I, along with Otis, of course. On the return trip, Otis stopped to "go to the bathroom," and Andy informed me that I was not supposed to watch him because he doesn't like that. Of course, I laughed and said, "*Ach*, Andy, you don't know." In all seriousness he said, "Oh yes, Mom, he wants to be left alone. I never look when he goes." So I suppose their understanding is mutual, and Otis will keep his privacy! The minute Andy comes home from school, he grabs a bite to eat, and it's off with Otis, doing chores, checking traps, and of late, siccing him on poor Becky's beloved cats. They're so fat and pampered, and absolutely despise Otis. Andy gets this wicked glee to watch Otis chase these poor, fat, nervous cats. As soon as Otis spies one, it's a hot speed race for the barn, with Andy yelling for Otis to go for it. If Becky happens to encounter this unfair spectacle, she charges out the door, screeching at Andy and pounding him with a fury. Andy hangs on to his hat, and silently laughs. Whose side do I choose, Becky and the cats, or Otis 'n' Andy? May the best man win (sigh).

[JANUARY 9, 1995]

Smack!

Last week we scootered to a neighboring pond with a thermos of hot chocolate, some snacks, a sleeping bag, and our skates. I had almost forgotten how much fun skating is. There was just enough snow to make it almost dangerous, because when you fell, there was no sliding. Poor Anna, who is eight, came crying, and she claimed she fell so hard there is a full person imprint on the ice. After wiping tears and a cup of good hot chocolate, we skated over to investigate. Sure enough, there was a perfect figure of one little girl's arms and legs outstretched!

[JANUARY 17, 1995]

Guilty Until Proven Innocent

Something killed and partially ate one of Andy's precious pigeons. He is suspicious of Becky's cats, and there is no mercy anywhere for the poor, unsuspecting, fat cats. He is furious and told Becky this morning he is setting a trap and if it's one of Becky's cats, that's just tough. They argued and discussed it until I was thoroughly tired of it. Laura sat patiently chewing her breakfast toast and just quietly rolled her eyes in exasperation. Becky told Andy she feeds her cats faithfully every morning with fresh water and cat food. They're fat and "would never eat your stupid pigeons anyway." Andy loudly informed her that, of course, only a fat cat wouldn't eat the whole pigeon and he's going to shoot them both. Whose side am I on? I don't know and I want to be fair to both.

Sometimes motherhood is so wearisome. You just don't always know what's best. That's when you appreciate your husband and his wisdom. Tonight at the supper table, the argument resumed, till Gid put a stop to it, saying he is tired of eating cats for supper!

[JANUARY 17, 1995]

Going to School

Today I was at the sewing machine with only Emily for company. Rosanne and her little cousin Mary went along to school today. Mary was not enthused about school at all, so Ruthie felt a day with our girls might get her accustomed to the ways of a school. Our girls were just bubbling over when they got home, because Mary was such a brave little girl. Mary was astounded to learn that teacher Marianne speaks Dutch and she just loves her now. The little Mennonite girls all made up well with her too.

Emily is not used to playing alone and today she surprised me so much. She has a vivid imagination, as she had an imaginary puppy she played with. She would lift the skirt of the couch, peep underneath and tell her puppy to come out. She carried this invisible dog around the kitchen and set dishes of imaginary food out for him. I asked her what his name is and she said, Trooper, which is Israel's golden Lab. She's terrified of him because of his huge size. She probably figured she'll play with him as long as he's not here!

[JANUARY 17, 1995]

"Vain on da Green Grass"

All I can think of this morning is the poem the girls taught Rosanne, who is four, and she still has trouble pronouncing her words, especially r's.

They play school constantly right now, and hold a program almost every other day. They sing and recite poems, and Rosanne just loves it. This is what she says ("v" for "r"): Vain on da green grass; Vain on da trees; Vain on da top-house (meaning housetop); Vain not on me!

And she said it so loudly and with such a big smile that we could hardly contain ourselves. Now everyone is repeating it all over the place, and it's all I can think of this morning.

Our children always have something they keep repeating, sometimes it's funny and other times it's so provoking. I guess children have always had their own special sense of humor, and it adds spice.

[JANUARY 24, 1995]

Oh, My Gosh!

Childhood was such an innocent time. My memory is not the best, and one of my earliest is of a neighbor lady, Mildred Bixler, who lived in the town of Greble in Lebanon.

She said, "Oh, my gosh," to Mom, and I thought this sounded so classy. So when Eva and I sat out in our playhouse eating our snack, I said, "Oh, my gosh," to Eva and she scolded me thoroughly and with so much conviction that I was sure God would never forgive me.

Eva was like that, always saying her prayers and her conscience bothered her sorely, and I hopped into bed and fell blissfully asleep and things never bothered me much. I guess we are all born with a different nature, and later in life, when things become serious, that is our biggest challenge, that big "self." But somewhere along the way we discover the love of our good Lord Jesus, and His forgiveness and mercy, and that is what makes everything so worthwhile. The burdened parents raising a large family with many cares, what makes the load lighter than the remembrance of Him? That's what lets the spirit grow lighter, and a song emerges.

For He knows and understands, and cares deeply about every one of us. If He wouldn't, I would be the very least to even think of heaven.

[JANUARY 24, 1995]

All's Forgiven

Life is so quiet. I don't even have an Otis and fat cat incident, and no more half-eaten pigeons. The cats curl up peacefully on the picnic table and calmly eat their cat food. Otis stays down in the barn with the heifers and calves.

Andy and Becky must have thoroughly forgiven each other, as they were helping each other with vocabulary and English last evening, the best of buddies.

[JANUARY 24, 1995]

Brought Down to Size

Yesterday we had buddies' day at Christ Lapps. She had a very pretty dark green and burgundy "Double Wedding Ring" quilt in frame, so the day flew by, with many hands quilting. The day was a bit more serious than usual, and I felt so privileged to be there again. Sometimes we're afraid we talk too much, but sharing and caring about each other's failures, disappointments, etc. is so vital to the life of a community. Sometimes laying down your pride and admitting mistakes is hard, but there is always a great blessing in that.

Anyway, I was just starting to climb up on top of my famous pedestal, ready to start waving my flag, when I was openly reprimanded on the front page of *Die Botschaft*. Back down I went, and now I'm relaxed again!

Thank you, whoever it was, because I kind of wondered if I should write that, and usually "when in doubt, don't" is the best. Perhaps I'm trying to show off about Otis and Andy, and I needed that.

[FEBRUARY 9, 1995]

Health Issues

I'm traveling across the mountains with an old neighbor lady every two weeks to see my good friend, Lydia Byler. I trust her a little better with her foot reflexology since she doesn't make me fly right off the recliner anymore.

My stomach problems came from a hiatal hernia, and she did a wonderful job, and fixed me right up. I love to go over there, just relax and talk about many different subjects. I'm not a "health nut" or strictly "medical," I just believe both fields have their time and place, and try and use common sense with both. She does have a God-given talent, and I really appreciate it when my stomach "kicks up."

[FEBRUARY 9, 1995]

Cough—Permission to Type

Teacher Marianne has an electric typewriter and if one of the girls has a cough or a cold, they may stay inside and use it. That Becky is so desperate to stay inside so she may type that she keeps coughing and coughing every morning. I can tell it's not a really serious cough, so one evening this week she coughed extra hard and said, "Mom, aren't you listening how hard I'm coughing?"

Yes, I surely was, and thinking she'd actually make a good actress.

[FEBRUARY 9, 1995]

See Ya, Otis

I don't want to show off or bore people about Otis. But the other morning I saw Andy standing at the door, waving and talking to someone. He was saying, "See you later," etc. And there sat Otis, on top of the picnic table, his head cocked to one side, listening intently to what Andy was saying. Otis always follows Andy up from the barn, and knows that it's time for him to go to school. He said this morning he dreamed last night we were going to take Otis from him, and he was planning on running away from home. He could hardly talk; I think the dream was so real. I assured him we would never, ever do that to him.

[FEBRUARY 9, 1995]

Perfect Ice

Laura, Andy, and I scootered down to Paul Bert's pond to check the ice this evening. Smooth as glass with big deep cracks in it. Just perfect. There's a beautiful full moon tonight and Andy wanted to go after supper, but I have no baby-sitter this evening. So he told us all what he thinks of us, then pouted on the couch, looking as fierce as Papa Bear. Laura proceeded to lecture him on the fine art of giving up your own will, finishing with, "That's all that's wrong with you." This started another barrage of unhappy words from Andy. I let it all cool down and ignored him, and soon they all decided to go across the fields to Watson's little pond, happily and peacefully. They've been there for the past hour, so they must be enjoying themselves.

[FEBRUARY 13, 1995]

Yum, Yum…

We attended the Horse and Buggy Mennonite Church at Clearfield. It was interesting to attend church at Clearfield. Daniel Zimmerman had the opening and Alvin Zimmerman delivered the main sermon. Ervin Zimmermans invited us for dinner, along with Alvins, Daniels, and Enos Z.'s. Lucy's dinner was as delicious as I had anticipated, as she's a talented cook. Homemade filled doughnuts dusted with powdered sugar, huge meatballs swimming in a tangy sauce, and scalloped potatoes. Everything was so good. I whispered to Laura, "Let's forget about our fat grams today and enjoy it."

I wanted to write about our new way of eating, but she says absolutely not, so I'll respect her wishes.

[FEBRUARY 23, 1995]

Visiting

Joe Blank's David was here with Andy for the weekend. Joes, Emanuel Stoltzfuses, and Amos Blanks were in Gettysburg over Sunday and David wanted to stay here. He's so quiet and was well-behaved and no trouble at all. Andy and David ate a whole cake, a yellow one with chocolate icing!

Laura and Becky were delighted when Emma King asked them to come for the weekend. Ikes had gone to Lancaster with Bennie K. Fishers and their Stevies, so Joe and Emma were alone with the chores.

They enjoyed themselves and fussed and fussed and fussed when they got home. Well, Becky did most of it. Laura is usually more reserved. She had this horror story of their neighbor's gigantic chocolate Lab named Max, and if you walked really slowly he kept his distance, and if you didn't he jumped on you; and how much butter Joe uses when he makes popcorn; and how cute the workhorse's colt is, and on and on.

[FEBRUARY 27, 1995]

Ouch! That Burns

Israel's Mose, who is fifteen, had an accident when he threw a bit of black gunpowder on a small fire to make it burn. He forgot he was holding a small container in his other hand, and it exploded. He has second-degree burns over much of one side of his face, and his hair is not where it used to be! He was in quite a bit of pain by the time he got to the emergency room, but said yesterday it just feels tight, and isn't very painful. He's always had a fascination with explosive things, inventing "cannons," etc. but as he certainly would agree, it doesn't take much to get hurt!

Dan Esh's Ervin cut his one finger almost off on a saw in the shop where Dan builds bird feeders, mailboxes, etc. Gid said they reattached it, so hopefully he'll be able to use it again. Maybe Mose and Ervin should have buddies' day this week!

[FEBRUARY 27, 1995]

A Cold Outing

Housecleaning continues, after not accomplishing too much last week because of circumstances.

Wednesday I put Emily in the scooter basket, and

Rosanne stood in front of me. We enjoyed an early morning scooter ride to David Flauds, where Ike King sei Sarah and I helped Sarah Flaud quilt. She sure has a talent to use scraps of material and turn them into old-fashioned quilts and wall hangings. I enjoyed my day so much, and seemed it was so special just us three old "buddies." Coming home, a cold wind blasted us directly in the face, and it just kept pushing us back, it seemed like. I was exhausted, and poor Emily's teeth were chattering. I had the girls really bundled up, but the wind was fierce. Emily claimed she was frozen and couldn't walk or talk when we got home! Rosanne loved all the attention from Laura and Becky and thought it was a big adventure. She probably felt like she had conquered the North Pole or something.

[MARCH 28, 1995]

Grinning Canine

Do dogs smile? Andy and Laura declare Otis smiles when he's pleased. His eyes turn down at the sides and he pulls his mouth back till there are two wrinkles. They're playing baseball and Otis is in his glory. His tail is constantly wagging, round and round, and he's having a wonderful time. Sunday forenoon I heard Andy seriously hollering, and there he lay, facedown with both hands over his head. Otis stood on top of Andy, biting his head, and Andy was in helpless giggles. "*Do net*, Otis. *Do net*." He twisted himself around and they wrestled and rolled and Otis was "smiling" all the while.

[MARCH 28, 1995]

Oh, That Food!

I forgot to mention that Elmer Fisher sei Lydia invited her Kauffman sisters and their daughters. We knotted comforters, made "Tumbling Block" couch covers and curtains. And we ate. Oh, grrrr! What to do on a day like that? Everyone brought a dish, and between the creme de menthe bars and the pies, casseroles, and pudding, it was hopeless. Ruthie grinned and loaded her plate, quietly telling me she's eating what she wants and as much as she wants. I heartily agreed.

[MARCH 28, 1995]

Minus 40 Pounds

I was reminded how I failed to mention that Emanuel and Maryann were at Ben Kurtzes in church awhile back. Oh my, did I really do that? How could I possibly forget? Well, I did, and the only excuse is that there's hardly anything left of Maryann, and Emanuel sat with the men in the living room where I couldn't see him!

Maryann honestly lost forty pounds with the Shape-Rite products, as did Sarah Kurtz. Yes, I'm envious. Who wouldn't be? But since we're not supposed to covet our neighbor's "figure,"

I'll still be nice to them, because I have to. In all seriousness, they're among my favorite aunts and I love them dearly.

[APRIL 14, 1995]

Surprise!

My thoughts go more toward Peter Abe Weavers again since yesterday, when a van load of Mom's relatives came to surprise her on her 60th birthday. And a genuine surprise it truly was!

Paul Miller Betty wrote about two weeks ago, so we planned on having sisters' day at Moms, and they would come around 10:00. Mom was putting clean sheets on Dad's bed when someone said, "Here comes a load of company." Mom thought, "*Ach*, my," because all us girls were home for the day! And it was her beloved relatives, Henry Hershbergers, Fred Hershbergers, and Paul Millers and their Amy and Michael. They brought a huge birthday cake and a delicious dinner, and we girls supplied the supper. Mom could relax and sit with Vern all day and they shared Grandma Weaver's scrapbook and talked.

Junior brought one of his hedgehogs down for Vern to see, and we won't say what she said, but she sure didn't like it! She claimed it looks like a rat and she detests them. So it was a special, special day, and none of us will forget Mom's 60th birthday.

Dad tried to start singing "Happy Birthday," but he choked up after a few words, 'cause Mom was crying, so we never even sang "Happy Birthday."

[APRIL 19, 1995]

Girls' Day Out

Lots of visiting was done on Easter Monday. We were invited to Ben Eshes, and David Flauds, but Gid was in a bind with book work, so he worked on that. Andy went fishing all by himself, with Otis, across the green hills, and he was perfectly happy. So the five girls and I went for a long scooter ride. First to the post office in Roxbury, then to the store for sandwiches, etc., and to the playground where I appliquéd and the little girls had so much fun, sliding, swinging, and racing around.

[APRIL 19, 1995]

Signs of Spring

Eli Dad's horse is due to have a colt, so they went with us to communion. Big old Charlie has no problem pulling a load over the hills we travel to Middle Springs.

. . . . .

Dad's four nanny goats have thirteen kids among them! They're so cute, and I often wonder if the mothers know whose baby is whose?

. . . . .

Bluebirds are back and they're building a nest. Andy's fishing wasn't too successful, so he came home early and built another birdhouse, room enough for three families, and set it on a pole.

. . . . .

Well, my appliquéing is waiting. Laura and I decided to do a big quilt for the Amish school sale, the second Saturday in May. It will keep me busy, but the girls can quilt, too. Laura actually does finer work than I do, but I tell her I go faster!

[APRIL 19, 1995]

Becky and Her Cats

I just finished bandaging Becky's knee, after she soaked it thoroughly in salt water. She went flying down the hill and Otis jumped out directly in her path. She swerved to avoid hitting him and ended up in a pile on the road. She does have one deep cut on her knee; otherwise, she was unhurt.

Her beloved cat with the sore foot was found in a nest with three baby kittens. She was so surprised and delighted that she cried. Finally she owns an orange kitten, and she is pleased beyond words. Even Andy felt all tender and helped arrange hay bales to keep Otis from pestering them.

[MAY 2, 1995]

Uh, Honey...

David and Emma Byler were our supper guests Sunday evening. Gid was supposed to tell me Thursday and remembered on the way to church. At times like these you just love your husband, don't you? Anyway, we had a simple supper with no fancy puddings or pie, and we thoroughly enjoyed our evening. Mom and Dad Byler joined us later.

[MAY 2, 1995]

Fishing

Levi Esh's Jesse and David picked up Andy and they went fishing in the creek at Pinola. They must have had a great time, 'cause Andy fell into the creek twice, chased mallard ducks and geese, and was simply exhausted. I had a feeling Levi's boys, the trout, ducks, geese, and fishworms all sighed a huge sigh of relief when Andy was safely home. He is so enthused and energetic. Sometimes I think he enjoys life twice as much as ordinary people.

[MAY 2, 1995]

Human Dog

I do believe Otis thinks he is human. He sits on the chairs on the porch, and swings with Andy on the porch swing. If Andy sits on a chair, Otis jumps up beside him, and they stare into space, contemplating their world and the future in general. Andy never mentions a brother anymore, and I believe Otis is a good companion.

[MAY 2, 1995]

Finally a Fence

I'm sitting down beside the barn, where Andy constructed a brand-new fence today. He wants to keep his baby ducks and geese here. He claims he couldn't sleep this morning, thinking about his wonderful day. The last day of school and finally, at long last, Gid gave him permission to build the fence. He's hard at work with a shovel, digging a little pond for them.

[MAY 9, 1995]

Mmmm...Rhubarb

I just finished planting tomatoes, and Andy helped me mulch them with hay. Now the garden is full, and things look productive. We're enjoying fresh onions and radishes, and so far I've begged two French rhubarb pies from people!

Mom Byler sent one over, and Monday at the quilting I told Bena she should make me one. And, of course, tonight on her way to Elmers, she stopped in with a still-warm, fresh-from-the-oven rhubarb pie. I dearly love them, and don't need them a bit, but that's beside the point.

Rhubarb only lasts a short while and I plan to enjoy every bite, dedicated dieter that I am!

[MAY 9, 1995]

A New Job

I decided today I suppose people let their children go by degrees. Laura's last day of school, and already she went to Elmers to work at the greenhouse. She's so totally different than I am. With hardly any self-confidence, and it's hard for her to meet new people, etc. I felt every bit as choked up as I did on her first day of school, to see her pack her lunch and go scootering off. I know she will be in excellent hands, as Elmers are nice people to work for. And I suppose I have to grow up yet, too, and learn to let the children face life by themselves. Sometimes I wish it would always stay this way, with all the children at home, in our big noisy house, but I know changes are necessary as life goes on.

[MAY 9, 1995]

Amish Swimming Pool

Andy's latest venture is so ridiculous, it's almost embarrassing to write about it. Since there are no hogs here on the farm, the concrete manure pit stood empty. Andy hatched this wonderful idea of cleaning it all out, and he even used the pressure washer to finish. He filled it with water, went fishing, and put his fish in the five-gallon bucket, dumping them in, and he has his own pond! Then he cut a big plastic barrel in two, and sits in this awkward-looking little tub and goes fishing. Even the little girls enjoy it, spending hours down there. Gid won't allow the water to become too deep, afraid that someone might fall in.

I told Andy all we need is some chlorine and a filter, and we'll have our own Amish swimming pool.

[MAY 9, 1995]

Double Blessings

Finally I can announce the birth of Emanuel and Rhoda Byler's twins! They arrived on Friday, a boy and a girl, weighing 3 lb. 10 oz. and 3 lb. 12½ oz. They remain at Hershey Hospital, but they are doing well, breathing on their own, and the doctors are well pleased. Their names are Roy James and Rosetta Jean. Rhoda came home Sunday evening, after almost eight weeks at Hershey, and she is doing well, although she's weak and a bit sore.

They walked over here last evening, after visiting the babies at Hershey, and they seem so happy that all is over, and Rhoda enjoys the fresh spring air most of all. They wish to extend a heartfelt "Thank You" for all the money, cards, letters, and sunshine box presents. I don't think we realize how it feels when people are such cheerful givers until we are on the receiving end. I'm sure they feel unworthy, and everyone has been so helpful.

On the same day the twins were born, *Doddy* Byler's horse had a baby colt, named Rose. All these babies, with fifteen baby goats as well. We should think of fifteen names starting with R for the goats: Rufus, Rachel, Robert, Richard, etc.!

It would be easier to name them all R.J. for Really Jumpy, 'cause that's about all they do.

[MAY 17, 1995]

New School

On Monday we scootered to Otterbein School to their picnic, as our children are planning on attending there next year. We've been undecided the last few years, and now we have decided to leave the Mennonite school. It's hard, because we have enjoyed Marianne Zimmerman as a teacher for all of Laura's eight years there.

[MAY 17, 1995]

Staining the Patio

A perfect day. Everywhere you looked, it was just a perfect day.

We made the most of it, doing a huge laundry, then putting two coats of Jason Fisher's stain on our patio. Mom and Ruthie came for coffee, and we handed Ruthie a brush and put her to work. Mom held the container of stain for me, and we talked a mile a minute before they left.

Then we worked in the garden the remainder of the day, so tonight it feels good to sit down.

[MAY 22, 1995]

Frozen Tongue

Tonight I got my tongue stuck hard against a twinsicle. You know, those icy popsicles we all loved when we were children. I bought a box from the Schwans man and wanted to show the girls that if you just let your tongue there it won't hurt. And it stuck. It hurts, too. So I went to the sink and let cold water run over the popsicle, tongue and all, and it felt horrible. I wonder what I said that caused it!

[MAY 22, 1995]

Andy Grows Up (a Little)

Andy is finally allowed to go on one of the crews and work this summer. He just loves it, and works with Ervin Zimmerman and Omar Stoltzfus.

They put equipment in turkey houses, and Andy helps carry pipes, assemble feeders, etc. Laura claims he's so "big feeling" that he can't talk right, but it's all in fun. I think we're all a little amazed that there is actually a chance of Andy growing up.

[MAY 22, 1995]

Big Black Bodyguard

That Otis. Emily went walking up from the barn all by herself, with Otis protecting her like a big black bodyguard. I asked Emily if she walked all the way by herself. She said, "No, Otis is here." And I told her Otis really likes her, and before I thought I said, "*Gel*, Otis?" He is just like a person. I felt extremely silly, and was so glad no one heard, but he is definitely one of the family. He kind of grows on you.

[MAY 22, 1995]

Painting...Otis

Good old summertime. Days are long and the sun is hot. The children are asking to go swimming every day, and the strawberries and peas are ready. We've been painting fence and even Otis was painted. No wonder. There he sat, his tail dragging against the freshly painted boards. Grrr! Everyone would holler for him to move, but there he sat, with no intentions of leaving.

[JUNE 6, 1995]

Yummy Wedding Meal

We returned safely from Ohio, arriving here at 3:15 on Wednesday morning. We enjoyed the wedding, and I will let the Geauga County scribes fill in all the proper details. I just know I've never eaten such scrumptious desserts. Yum! Yum! I know Ohio ladies love to bake and cook, but this was unreal. Strawberry tapioca pudding, all creamy and delicious. Pies, pies, pies, and great big layer cakes all over the place. I still wonder who made the German sweet chocolate with coconut frosting. I'd love to have the recipe.

I met with different scribes, and it was all very interesting. It was nice to be with the aunts again, and Becky Stoltzfus from Maryland.

[JUNE 6, 1995]

Cats and Dogs

Becky and Andy had an all-out royal feud this morning. Andy wanted Becky to move her kitties out of the granary and she refused. "No way, they're my cats." So Andy dumped a bunch of her cat food into the hay. To retaliate, Becky scrambled down the ladder and promptly dumped a whole pile of dog food all over Otis's dish. You could see their eyes snapping at each other across the table. No matter how smoothly this dog-cat thing goes, it's much like a volcano seething, and occasionally it erupts.

[JUNE 6, 1995]

Where Are the Toothbrushes?

Would the person who hid our toothbrushes and toothpaste please write us a letter or call and let us know where they are?

We've looked and looked and looked! I'm still curious who our company was, and I think you were very clever. A teddy bear sat in the middle of the bed with Gid's hat on, all his boots hung from pegs, chairs on top of the kitchen table, and lots of things rearranged. It was funny, but where are the toothbrushes? I'm blaming Jonathan Stoltzfuses from Addison, New York, as someone said they planned to stop in. Or Uncle Ben Stoltzfus from Lancaster, who had wanted to stop and see the twins. So come on, out with it!

[JUNE 6, 1995]

Food Preparations

I made my first strawberry jelly today, and put the berries, caps and all, through the Victorio strainer. Now whoever invented that idea was really smart. It was so easy to take that juice and add sugar and Sure-Jell and you have lump-free bright red jelly! I'll have to make a lot more.

I must run along and make a huge roaster of scalloped potatoes to take to Dad Kauffmans. They're having their annual shrimp supper tonight, and this little fatty is anticipating the aroma already. Woe is me when it comes to good food. But I did mow the whole yard in the hot sun, figuring that would help my metabolism take care of what I plan to eat.

I'm always defeating the purpose, because when I work hard I'm always mentally calculating how many cupcakes that amounted to!

[JUNE 6, 1995]

Tangled Peas

Does an abundance of peas and strawberries sound familiar, ladies? That's what most of us poor overworked souls are doing, right? This morning when we tackled twelve rows of "Green Arrows," soaking wet, cold, muddy, and sodden, I was having second thoughts about raising peas. Down one row and I was having more serious thoughts about love and marriage.

Seventeen years and Gid still doesn't believe in putting in stakes and wire to support the stalks. When do you give up for real? 'Cause I don't think I ever have. These stalks were so tangled and impossible to straighten out, and the longer I picked, the grouchier I got.

Every year it's the same. I never say much, and secretly admire myself for being so virtuous, and every pea-picking I get as mad as a hornet. I must have been fuming silently, because Laura quietly suggested we try Irma Zimmerman's way. She pounds in stakes and uses baler twine, then wraps it all up, stakes, twine, dead stalks, and all, and burns them.

[JUNE 13, 1995]

Roaming Dog

Otis became bored with life since Andy started working, so he found a friend. Across the field and through a small patch of woods lives a Saint Bernard named "Bub," and Otis decided Bub's dog food far surpasses his own. We had to spank, scold, watch, and go over to the neighbors and apologize about five times, but he stays home now. They think he's nice and named him "Fred." We didn't think it was funny, because it can be a real problem once they start to roam.

[JUNE 13, 1995]

Another Accident

Israel's Stephen fell off the pony cart last evening and the wheel went over his body. He landed on his head and they could tell he was hurt seriously, as he couldn't support his head. He had surgery last night, and they took a large blood clot off his brain. He'll be in ICU for a few days, but is doing as well as can be expected. Accidents happen so fast, and seemingly no one's fault, just an act of God to draw us closer to Him. Isn't it amazing how we depend on Him, and even more so in times of stress or sorrow?

[JUNE 13, 1995]

Training Otis

I'm up earlier than usual, trying to help Andy with training Otis to stay home. We've had a rough week, with Andy in desperation, trying to keep him home. He's wandering to neighbors who do not appreciate him at all. Gid decided to tie him up on Saturday and I don't know who cried more, Otis or Andy. Otis thought this was an outrage and almost hung himself. So we decided if we all work together and each one takes his share of the responsibility perhaps we can train him to stay at our command.

He never tries to go along anymore when we go away with the buggy, scooter, or whatever. But this may be more difficult.

[JUNE 20, 1995]

A Miracle

Israel Stoltzfus's Stephen is at home now, after his stay in the hospital. The doctors and nurses pronounced him a miracle, after massive bleeding on his brain from a tumble off the pony cart. After being taken to the emergency room, his condition was fairly stable, then suddenly he began fading rapidly. A CAT scan revealed a large blood clot forming, and they performed emergency surgery and saved his life. He's doing really well at home, but it's hard to keep him down. He's an active six-year-old and is getting bored. When we visited him at the hospital, he cocked one swollen little eye over at me and asked if I knew he almost died. I assured him that we had heard about it, and he blinked his eyes a couple times and smiled up at me as if it was absolutely amazing that he made it after all!

[JUNE 20, 1995]

Socializing Mommy

These three little girls simply make me feel guilty for not giving them more attention these days. They have their own little playhouse in a small room and they play constantly with their dolls.

Emily is either a mother or a baby, depending what the older ones decide she should be. If she is a mother, she'll stand at the kitchen wall and start to knock. And I'll say, "Come in, Ruthie," or Eva or whoever she is that day. So she'll take her doll and settle on the couch and we'll have a very adult visit. She always went shopping and her baby has an earache and she's busy these days. Then she'll put her baby carefully in the stroller and go home.

[JUNE 20, 1995]

"Blicking" Cherries

Saturday afternoon we went to *Doddy* Sam Z. Bylers in Gettysburg to finish her quilt—Dad Bylers, Ike King sei Sarah, and me. *Doddy* and Dad picked sour cherries and *Doddys blicked* them. How do you say that in English? Not "stoned" them, as that conjures up a picture of *Mommy* standing over the bucket of cherries with a large stone. I mean take out the pits. Anyway, if the cherry squeaks when you press it, there is a worm inside. Every time *Mommy* heard it, sure enough, there was a worm! You learn something every day.

We finished the quilt and I think *Mommy* was relieved, as she can barely see to sew at all anymore. Otherwise, they are well, still baking and going on their route, gardening, canning, etc.

[JUNE 27, 1995]

Where IS That Dog?

That Otis. What a huge problem he is! His love for his neighbors' dogs is becoming the biggest headache. Early in the morning he'll disappear and Andy will whistle and whistle. Here he comes, soaking wet, through the hay field, tongue lolling and "smiling" so happily. And the one set of neighbors does not appreciate him at all, because he chases their cat, which he was taught to do at home.

Oh, mercy, now what? Endless discussions always have the same result. Absolutely, Gid and Andy won't consider having him neutered. Andy will not tie him, and he insists he can be trained. What a frustrating few weeks! I have a permanent pucker in my upper lip from whistling, and all the cheese slices disappear, because that is the treat we give him for a reward. Andy tied him once, and I guess it's safe to say he's been staying home now for five days. So if visitors stop in, nine chances out of ten, I'll be eating a bologna sandwich without cheese and my mouth looks all wrinkled across the top. *Ach*, dogs, who needs them?

. . . . .

Oh, Yonie and Linda from Addison: We found our toothbrushes in the clothes hamper! I couldn't help but laugh. Here we were steadily covering them up, and running everywhere, searching in vain! Wish I could come hide your toothbrushes now.

[JUNE 27, 1995]

Grumbling Husbands

Ike King sei Sarah spent the afternoon with Mom Byler yesterday. Emma said they were busy with cucumbers Monday evening, so they put cereal on the table for supper, resulting in some grumbling from Ike and the boys. So yesterday they made a good meat and potatoes dinner, set the table with their good Sunday dishes, and left a note before leaving for Grandma's.

Gid probably wishes his grumping would bring such good response. It was much the same at our house. Knee deep in cucumbers, and I slammed warmed-up chicken noodle soup and barbeque on the table.

The soup was spoiled and I felt so awful, and Gid announced the barbeque was too spicy. So he ate cereal, and I threw my hands in the air and gave up. It was only the ending to a frustrating day. For starters, Laura had a dentist appointment, and they wouldn't pull the tooth which another dentist had said would correct her crowding. Forty dollars and nothing accomplished. After that, an unfruitful shopping trip for shoes, grouchy girls, hot weather, late till we got home, and piles of pickles to do. Enter the spoiled soup, spicy beef, and unhappy husband. I even went to bed early in case anything else might happen.

[JULY 12, 1995]

Remedied

The little twins weigh around 7 lb. and are eight weeks old. They've really gone through a lot, with both of them crying and having stomach problems. We kind of felt it was colic, as they cried almost constantly. But Rhoda insisted those babies don't feel well, and there must be something wrong. The pediatrician couldn't do much besides prescribe different formula, and the problem became steadily worse. In desperation, they took them to Joseph and Miriam Druist in Shirleysburg. They are "herbal" or "natural" people.

She saw they weren't feeling well, and said their little digestive systems aren't working. She treated them, gave them something for indigestion, and they stopped crying. She suggested goat's milk diluted with spring water, and only 2 oz., plus she gave them different things to aid their digestion.

The babies are very different now. I just couldn't believe how relaxed they were—sleeping soundly at night for three hours at a time, and the constant crying stopped. Needless to say, Emanuel and Rhoda were exhausted parents, getting a few hours of sleep every night. It's such a joy to see them all relaxed and smiling now.

[JULY 12, 1995]

Long Overdue Railing

Gid is working on the porch railing in the evenings. After waiting for five years, he's actually getting it accomplished, and needless to say, I'm so thrilled. The house is starting to look as I had imagined it when we built it. This porch railing really must be getting to me, because I dreamed an airplane wrecked into the corner post. It all came tumbling down, and I was so disappointed, because I figured it would take another five years for Gid to fix it. Oh well, pride goes before a fall, you know, and hopefully, all the airplanes will stay in the air in Franklin County.

[JULY 17, 1995]

Grandparents

I haven't been to Dads for about a week, then today I stopped in to pick up Laura and Becky. Rosanne just stood at the door, twitching her shoulders self-consciously, patiently watching *Mommy* Kauffman talk.

Soon *Mommy* caught sight of her, and with a resounding "Rosie!" she was enveloped in a huge warm grandmotherly hug. Rosanne's eyes shone like twin stars for the remainder of the ride home.

I hope my children always appreciate their grandparents. They receive so much love from each side of the family, and it makes you feel so unworthy. Grandparents' love is simply something that stays in your heart.

I can still remember *Doddy* Peter Abe Weaver so well. I was always so fascinated with all those blue and purple veins in his large nose, wondering what would happen if one burst. He would grab our necks with his wooden varnished cane. We would holler and try to struggle away, but we didn't much care.

We would push him to the small country store on his wheelchair and he would buy us all a huge ice cream sandwich. We just adored him! Now he's gone for a long time, but I still love to think of him.

[JULY 17, 1995]

Stung

I was peacefully taking down my wash when I was attacked by about three angry wasps. Normally I'm not afraid of them, except when they zoom in on you like fierce little bombers.

Well, I flapped an armful of towels, dancing around and screaming as loudly as I could. The girls came running to see what in the world was happening.

Andy attacked them with fly spray, and after things calmed down, Laura asked Becky where she was. Becky just rolled her eyes and said in a superior air that she was privileged to watch the whole show from her upstairs window. She shook her head and smiled in a sad way, much as if she was concerned for her mother's sanity.

Then yesterday, when the wonderful cool temperatures just lured me outside, we mowed, trimmed, and weeded our flower beds. I was bent over, minding my own business, when zap! three wasps stung me at one time. Ouch! It seems so unfair, because I didn't do anything to them, but I suppose if I was building a house under the basement ledge and a creature thousands of times bigger than me would come by, I'd defend myself too.

[AUGUST 8, 1995]

Otis Gets Painted Again

We finished painting the porch railing with oil-based high gloss enamel, which we thought would be the strongest paint. Poor Otis though. He got his back against the wet paint, and because we used naphtha gasoline to remove the paint from our hands, Andy thought it would work on Otis's coat.

Oh, my goodness, the poor dog almost went insane. He ran in circles as fast as he could with wild eyes, and was foaming at the mouth. It must have burned horribly 'cause he was clearly in terrible pain. So Andy lifted him to the watering trough in the barn, and sudsed him with every soap he could think of till he calmed down.

I'm glad when school starts, simply so Laura and I have more to do. She didn't have any work at Elmers since July, and there's just not enough to keep us both as busy as we should be. Buddies' day is here tomorrow, and I am planning on having three sewing machines going, to make shirts, etc. Well, they all claim they love sewing, so ...

[AUGUST 8, 1995]

Hot and Humid

I seriously wonder how many of us still have our good humor intact? It is uncomfortably humid, and even the girls, who are normally not fighters, just lie around on the couch, and beware if one touches the other.

We're cleaning for church, and while cleaning upstairs, I had very little patience. The slightest effort, and the perspiration starts rolling, along with your good humor and sweet nature. It really does make me feel unworthy at close of day that God forgives all our screeching and short temper and complaints.

[AUGUST 16, 1995]

Our Very Own Bear

Friday and Saturday we went camping at a place close to Mercersburg with Joe Blanks, Amos Blanks, and Jimmys. The "ladies" and children went Friday morning and our men joined us in the evening after work. That afternoon a thunderstorm broke, and we madly stuffed all our sleeping bags, blankets, food, etc. in Ruthie Flaud's little tent. Just as the rain poured down, we all ran for shelter in Ruthie's tent, and Barbie and Maryann sat in theirs! Of course, after Gid arrived, and swiftly set up ours, things went better. I forgot our gas lantern. The other campsites were lit up, toasting marshmallows with ease. Did you ever try to roast marshmallows in the dark with eight children? Andy was so mad, it was like having our very own bear. Gid sat on a lawn chair and just laughed at him.

[AUGUST 16, 1995]

A True Friendship

Andy scootered over to Levi Eshes to go swimming with their Jesse. Otis always gets the blues when Andy leaves. It was so hot, and he lay on the porch looking so sorrowful. Then he got up and walked to the edge of the yard, whining and looking expectantly down the road. About dark the girls said, "Otis, here comes Andy!" and he leaped up and sat at the very corner of the yard. He leaned forward so far that his nose was on the road. And what a reunion when Andy arrived! I'm not overly fond of his smell and some of his habits, but it would be a shame to break up a true friendship.

[AUGUST 16, 1995]

Cleaning the School

Dad Bylers are in Gettysburg today, at *Doddy* Sam Z.'s. *Doddy's* brothers are there, and we would have enjoyed going along, except we had the schoolhouse cleaning to do.

Lots of parents gathered at Otterbein School last evening. It's an old schoolhouse, with two rows of enormous windows with old-fashioned unhandy panes and storm windows. I was kept busy cleaning the desk, file, and bookcases, but it brought a few chuckles to see all those men diligently washing windows.

It was dark when we left, so I'm anxious to return on Thursday to survey that sparkling schoolroom. I'm even privileged to have a huge coal-burning stove that comes from the Gettysburg school. Dan sei Suzanne assured me I will really like it, and I'm so grateful for the stove.

Who could ever forget that drafty, cold schoolroom, no fire started, stove smoking? All the children kept their coats on and we marched around to warm our feet!

The girls and I want to spend all day there on Thursday, duplicating, sorting books, etc.

[AUGUST 22, 1995]

Slippery Kisses

Emily was so sweet and warm and sleepy this morning when she came downstairs.

I cuddled her and gave her a big kiss, which she promptly wiped off. I asked her why, and she looked at me so scornfully and said it's too slippery! She is three now and has a mind of her own. Yesterday Laura gave her one of her old harmonicas. She blows rapidly back and forth, accompanied by her head wagging and her feet stomping in unison.

[AUGUST 22, 1995]

Too Many Felines

Poor Becky. The mama cat had another litter of four kittens, and she tries to be as pleased as she was with the first. But there are too many cats! She put two in a box and gave them to Shorty's girls, but she still has a bunch.

Otis would gladly reduce the cat population for her, I'm sure.

. . . . .

Otis stays home now. Sometimes he goes down to the pasture with the horses, but he very seldom disappears.

[AUGUST 22, 1995]

Back to the Books

School is on, and I'm not sure if I should add an exclamation mark or just a period. Perhaps a question mark would convey my feelings the best.

The children are so sweet, and it makes me feel all the more inadequate. Their freshly scrubbed faces, all smiles and eager to please the new teacher, just went for my heart. It's just no wonder the Bible says we should all become as little children. They are, indeed, so precious.

Today was our first day of having actual work, and with 31 pupils there wasn't a dull moment.

I think it will go better once I get my act together! Talk about a dud. First, we colored name charts, and the upper grade boys wondered about using a black marker on top of red and yellow crayon. Yes, I assured them airily, it'll work. Well, it didn't. I messed up a whole pile of name charts before I gave up. Laura duplicated a bunch more, and we stenciled the name on first. Now the pupils have to color all over again. Plus, these new workbooks are so confusing. Which book goes with which reading book? I thought the upper graders seemed a little concerned about my stupidity today. Oh well, we'll work it out.

[AUGUST 29, 1995]

No Use Crying Over Spilled Milk

We spent Sunday at home. It was so warm, and it seemed all day everyone got on someone else's nerves. It was one of those Sundays that you are glad for Monday morning. Anyway, Andy spilled a gallon of milk all over the refrigerator and the floor. The inside of the refrigerator, where all the little bottles and Tupperwares are. Oh, grrr. I almost blew a fuse, but calmly got the paper towels and proceeded to clean up. Gid got up from his long nap on the couch, and clicked his tongue, smiled, and said, "That's what you get for complaining. Now you'll have plenty to do." I think I could cheerfully have hit him with a baseball bat right at that moment.

[AUGUST 29, 1995]

A Head of Corn?

Laura was sound asleep one morning and she felt this irritating pull on her hair. Just a little tug here and there. Finally she could no longer bear it, and sat up. There was Emily, her little bed-partner, wide awake. She informed Laura that she was doing corn. It didn't do much for Laura's ego, that her hair resembles corn silk.

[AUGUST 29, 1995]

Teacher Woes

Today was the first whole day of school.

Katie Yoder, by the end of the week I was almost ready to admit I should have listened to you. I suppose I thought I was a good teacher; this would all be a breeze, no problem. But even the books confused me!

So many new workbooks, the children all needed help, my classes were not going smoothly, and the clock just zipped around, leaving me totally frustrated. After a rather unruly art class on Friday, I had a lump in my throat as big as a walnut. Hot, dusty, and tired, fighting despair, Becky and I trudged up the hill, pushing our scooters. I sadly lamented to Becky how I just felt like a complete failure.

In all the wisdom she had gathered in her eleven years, she gave me the most pitying glance and said, "*Ach*, Mom, it's just the first week. Everybody is trying to impress each other. They'll all settle down." That cheered me up immediately for some reason.

So, onward we go, chin up, positive attitude, and never, ever, forget to ask the good Lord for strength for each day.

Today my self-esteem is bolstered again after a very good arithmetic class. But, oh, I could use a helper. Would I start a major controversy if I wondered aloud about all these workbooks? Are they really for the best? Teaching used to be so much more simple, and we had time for poems, compositions, etc., or is it just fat, weary, 37-year-old me? Probably, because when I walk down the aisles I scrape off everyone's notebooks, papers, etc.!

[SEPTEMBER 4, 1995]

Mighty Hunter

Gid went goose hunting this evening and dove hunting on Friday and Saturday, and I told him tonight he keeps getting worse and worse! He just grinned and said it's the time of year to gather the meat for the winter. I kind of choked back my snort, as I am improving somewhat on being a good submissive wife. The meat so far was a goose that was so stringy and greasy they threw it out and carefully washed all the greasy dishes. Dove breasts are a great delicacy to these Indians, meaning Gid and Andy. I always cook them and the whole kitchen smells like liver. Oh well, I'm so meek and mild and submissive, so…

[SEPTEMBER 4, 1995]

That Dog!

Emanuel and Rhoda came over last evening, and we thoroughly enjoyed the twins. Rosetta charmed us all with her smiles and gurgles, while Roy slept peacefully on our bed. The girls and I weren't aware that we had company, as we had gone on a real "Otis" hunt. Saturday evening he disappeared and all day Sunday we kept hoping he'd return. This morning there was still no Otis and we all felt a bit heartsick, although I was so tired of worrying about keeping him home, I kind of hoped that he had disappeared. He stayed home faithfully for a long time, but since school started, he's going on real adventures.

Joe Blank's David brought him home, and Jr. Esh sei Becca chased him out of their yard, and now where do you think he was over the weekend? He was about a mile away, at Levi Kings and Elmer Fishers. Levi said he went out on the porch to go do chores and there stood this huge black dog, growling menacingly. He had no idea whose it was! He woke up in a hurry. Then he chased Elmer's cats through their thousands of potted chrysanthemums, knocking them over as he went. Oh, woe is us! What an embarrassment! This well-trained, beloved Otis that I brag about every week in my letter has brought shame and disgrace on our heads. Oh well, I suppose pride always goes before a fall, and I guess we all needed it. So tonight, while Andy battled his tears, Gid said this is it, he must stay tied at night and while we're at school.

And he will hopefully be neutered in the near future. Why do our dogs always seem to have one major bad habit?

[SEPTEMBER 11, 1995]

School Days

My head is spinning, my legs are sore, and I'm tired and much busier than I ever imagined. But I'm loving every minute of it!

Truthfully, I completely forgot the thrill of a good, solid bat connecting with a softball and racing madly for first base. Or standing behind this old brick schoolhouse swinging a jump rope with the girls, singing, "Mabel, Mabel, set the table."

We have a beautiful view of the Blue Mountain from the school, and it always puts fresh *mut* into my heart to look at this beloved mountain.

Generations come and go at Otterbein, and the faithful mountain always stands guard. "I will lift mine eyes unto the hills from whence cometh my help."

Laura and Becky were checking English books, and it's absolutely a fright. They are into a serious fist fight, with Becky calling Laura an old "cow." Now it's no sense. I hollered and told them to shape up. The argument was about Becky's "imperative" sentence. It's wrong, and she's sure it isn't. Sigh.

[SEPTEMBER 11, 1995]

Let's Go!

Last evening we had a van load of Mennonite company from Barnett, Missouri, along with Lawrence Martins from Shippensburg, Amos Zimmermans, Paul Zimmermans, and Paul Shirks.

It was quite interesting to hear of their westward movement twenty-five years ago to that area. They were the first, and now there are 160 families.

It sure took courage, and I marveled at these ladies' staunch spirit. Gid was getting all excited, I could tell, 'cause he took his glasses off and cleaned them! Land taxes and prices for homes sound like a dream! I better work on my "submission" project awhile yet!

[SEPTEMBER 18, 1995]

Home Run Hitter

School is going fairly well. We're learning together, and everyone is relaxed and seems to accept me well. I'm still scootering and playing baseball. I even bought a new left-handed glove, as years ago I gave mine to Jake Stoltzfus when I quit teaching at Sunset School. Do you still have it, Jake? Today I hit three home runs. I don't know what I look like, but I sure am having fun!

[SEPTEMBER 18, 1995]

Teacher by Day, Mother by Night

Time to start housecleaning soon. Oh dear, when will we do it? Probably a room every evening. I come home and flop my 30 pounds of workbooks on the table and Laura goes to work on them, and I'm the mother—cooking, sewing, etc. Tonight I washed piles of laundry, and they checked English, vocabulary, and German. It's quite a life.

I have little Post-it notes on my desk that say: "There must be a method to this mess," with a frustrated cat almost covered with stacks of paperwork. Fits exactly!

[SEPTEMBER 18, 1995]

The "Lost" License

We did three bushels of smokehouse apples on Monday evening and cleaned two rooms upstairs on Saturday afternoon. So you can see, we just do our work at unusual times!

After firmly telling Gid he must let me sort through his hunting room, clean it, and move some things to the attic, he relented, but only with serious warnings about his doe license.

Losing his '95 doe license would be much like losing a precious belonging. In plain words, you don't mess with Gid's hunting things.

So, feeling a little bold, we hid it, and, of course, when he got home he asked, "Where is that white envelope?" In all innocence, I asked which envelope he meant. Well, he bounded up the stairs, and we all waited to see how loud things would become. They increased in intensity, and we started to giggle. After a few serious bangs, he came down and demanded that envelope. There was no hiding it after Andy burst out laughing.

[SEPTEMBER 27, 1995]

Overworked "Horsie"

I can't remember ever having such a laugh as we did the other evening while Laura, Becky, and I did dishes. Going across the lawn, looking so ludicrous, was little skinny Rosanne pulling the big express wagon. On the wagon they had two little chairs, one directly in front of the other. Chubby eight-year-old Anna sat on the front chair "driving" skinny overworked Rosanne.

On the back seat sat Emily, her vision completely obscured by Anna's wide back. She was singing as loudly as she could, her knee thumping up and down in time to her song. She was gazing first to the right, and then to the left, and straight up to the sky, completely engrossed in her singing.

To the three of us, who know Emily's strange little personality, it was quite the most hilarious scene. I managed to squeak to Laura to look out the window, and we simply hung onto the countertop and wiped tears until it was over.

[SEPTEMBER 27, 1995]

Lessons from Little Ones

School is going fairly well. I think I enjoy teaching, and the days fly by. We seem to have a noisy schoolroom, but I try to console myself by saying there are 35 with Emily and Rosanne. I just wish I could describe and introduce you to all my pupils. As time goes on, their special little personalities are such a constant joy. It seems the love of the children is such a delight.

I even felt guilty already to think I'm being paid to do something that doesn't seem very much like a job. Oh, I get tired and am sometimes grouchy in the morning, to get everyone on their scooter and down the road by 7:30.

But I never realized how seriously I would have

to fight back the humorous side, keep a perfectly prim, straight face, and calm everyone with a reprimand, when it would feel so good to laugh. Children are such a constant form of innocence, and we'd do so well to learn from them.

[SEPTEMBER 27, 1995]

School for Teachers

We attended teachers' classes at Mary Zook's school in Perry County on Friday evening. I felt very foggy and slightly out of place with all these "professionals," but, oh well, I'll learn. If I keep going to teachers' classes, I'll soon be a *chite* teacher.

I'm actually too busy to be sitting here writing. We housecleaned Anna's room this evening, and washed curtains and bedspreads.

It's almost bedtime, and after going for a hike in the woods with the children today, I'm ready to crash.

[OCTOBER 2, 1995]

Painful Molding Process

Bright blue October skies, chilly mornings, and perfect full moon at night. Who could ask the Creator for anything more beautiful? It makes you feel like going on a hayride and roasting hot dogs and marshmallows over a roaring fire.

Housecleaning, tests, report cards, the recent rains, yard growing, and piles of laundry. Help! Last week was a bit frustrating and that's just being polite. The honest truth, it was a fright. I'm not a very patient, submissive person when circumstances are beyond my control. I tend to snap and growl at Gid, scream at the children, and just make life miserable for us all.

This morning I finally reached a measure of peace by realizing I must now let the Master mold me into a different piece of "pottery." I have always been an organized, planned, everything-gets-done-at-certain-times kind of housekeeper. And we can't do that anymore. How do you give up your ways? It's so hard to change.

But, always, when I go to school, it's therapeutic. I love to teach. And no matter how grouchy I feel in the morning, I always feel revitalized at the end of the day. It's the children, I suppose, and my own dear ones. They have so much patience with their erring mom, and are always so ready to forgive.

[OCTOBER 9, 1995]

Filled to Capacity

Mom, Eva, Ruthie, Barbie, and I went to Lancaster on Saturday, shopping and doing different business. I always enjoy those days, and this time it was extra special, as I don't see my mom and sisters as much anymore. We always manage to fill a van to capacity, and everyone is less than comfortable the 100 miles home. We decided Eva isn't Billy Beaver after all—that it was the rabbit that kept complaining to the beaver in the reading—and she has earned her reputation. She says she's improving, though!

[OCTOBER 9, 1995]

Good-bye, Otis?

Poor Otis. He's turning into a disgrace to the Byler household. Running off as soon as we don't carefully watch him. Last night a man from Lurgan brought him home, and we apologized for the trouble. Andy just sat on the couch and stared at the floor. I asked if he doesn't want to sell Otis and get a female puppy, and with the most heartfelt, "Mom, I just can't," I could understand. He gets a big lump in his throat to even imagine parting with Otis. So, we'll see.

[OCTOBER 9, 1995]

Otterbein's Tom Sawyer

The girls are checking English books, and I have Christmas plays to write before teachers' class at Arie Stoltzfus's school Friday afternoon. We had wash to fold and put away. I washed again this evening and filled the lines with bedding, etc.

Things aren't like we were used to, but I feel so much better again. I guess I'm too proud to be sloppy, call it what you want, but I'm not happy if everything piles all over me.

We decided tonight that Laura will just stay home every day with the little ones. It's too cold for Emily to sit in the basket of the scooter.

And I honestly do question the need of a helper. The children are doing so much better with their workbooks after the first six weeks are over.

And I'm kind of getting into my own routine, and everything is going so much better. If I don't watch it, I will even start to like those English books—especially for first grade. They're just great for sounds and word starters.

I hesitate to use names to relate incidents in school, but oh, I would just love to share some happenings with all of you.

Last week one day this little girl's mom baked her a little pumpkin pie. She stood beside my desk eating it, spoonful after spoonful. It did look so mouth-wateringly delicious! Our school's "Tom Sawyer" was the casual observer, calmly watching her shovel in one succulent mouthful after another.

After awhile, he couldn't stand it anymore and cocked up one eyebrow, and sarcastically remarked, "I could easily eat that in one bite." The little girl's mouth dropped open, and she just couldn't believe it. "One bite?" The little boy walked away, as if to say, "What's so great about pumpkin pie?" and shot back, "Well, maybe three!"

I don't think a day goes by that I couldn't write a short story about one person or the other. Especially our Tom Sawyer!

[OCTOBER 16, 1995]

Laryngitis

What a drizzly, muddy morning to be scootering to school! Night crawlers all over the road made traveling conditions quite unappetizing. I heard Becky tell Anna if she drives over one worm, she's gonna *cutz*!

Along with the rain and the mud, I've acquired a genuine dose of laryngitis which reduces my speaking to a mere whisper or an unnerving grating squeak. Gid said he wishes it would get worse, so I'd be quiet. The children at school are so sweet and understanding, though. The big boys grin a little and say, "What?" but everyone seems to be sympathetic. I gave them review pages in arithmetic to eliminate unnecessary speaking, and we had no story time.

[NOVEMBER 2, 1995]

Important Visitors

On Wednesday of last week a van load of Lancaster *Botschaft* scribes came to visit school. I should have brought my guest book along home, because now I can't even write everyone's name. Anyway, when they said who they were, I started to feel very small indeed. I mean these people were honest-to-goodness, real, *chite* scribes, people whose letters amount to something and they're important. Knowing who everyone was, oh, I would gladly have crawled under my desk. Anyway, being green at having proper visitors, I had to call the children back in so the men could speak to the children. And what interesting speeches! The children talked about John Glick's steam whistle for quite a while. Benuel Fisher, I gave the children their candy for saying poems and flashcards. But I'm happy to tell you, after you left I ate all the circus peanuts myself while checking English books! Thank you! The peanut butter cookies were delicious. I ate three because I skipped lunch.

The biggest news is that Levi Esh's David found the answer to the arithmetic problem Sam put on the blackboard. He's in sixth grade, and he was very happy to receive the dollar bill.

Thank you again, over and over, for coming!

[NOVEMBER 2, 1995]

Sunup to Sundown

This week, after Gid moved his office home and we decided to do the book work, I thought I had to quit teaching altogether. The amount of paperwork from the previous five crews looked a bit overwhelming, and we decided I would just quit. It was so awful. I cried myself into a raging headache, while Andy and Becky looked like ghosts, just sadly sitting and staring into space. I just couldn't stand up there at my desk and tell the children I'm quitting. I tried to think of the bad things, but the children's expressions and innocent ways just overwhelmed me. Who would care for their feelings if I wasn't there? So many of them are so tenderhearted, and

I just couldn't stand it. So we decided between Laura and me, with the children pitching in, we'll survive if I go on. My days go something like this: School all day, come home at 4:15, mow, trim, and clean the yard, make supper, do dishes, cook mush for Gid's breakfast, pay bills, write a *Botschaft* letter, and as soon as Gid returns, we'll do book work down in the office.

Laura does all the washing, cleaning, etc. and helps with the book work. It's a fulfilling life, and I can't imagine being bored.

Otis, last but far from least, is roaming free again. He hasn't left at all since his stay at the vet's, and it's so nice to be relaxed about good old Otis. He was in the house when it was cold last weekend, and I kind of liked it.

[NOVEMBER 2, 1995]

The Busy Bees

Becky and her cousin, Becca Blank, and Marianne Fisher started a club called the Busy Bees. They made some papers on the duplicator and dropped them in neighbors' mailboxes. They'll rake yards, do dishes, and clean up for a small fee. When they have $20.00, they'll get pizza from Lynch's, a local deli! Can you imagine? I told Becky I'd get something worthwhile. Anyway, they cleaned up for Mom Kauffman and have a yard to rake at Amos Eshes tomorrow. It's so cute!

. . . . .

Good night. You can tell I have laryngitis. I write too much if I can't talk.

[NOVEMBER 2, 1995]

Communication—Zero

Well, we're finding out our family is still adjusting to having me teach school. Whenever I get grouchy at home, Gid says I'm not allowed to teach. And I pity myself because he isn't very supportive sometimes. So things got to the point where we cheerfully ignored each other for awhile and communication was down to zero. You know, the old silent treatment felt just fine, because I felt like I deserved a bit more understanding and support. So we had a real family conference after I realized my self-pity didn't hold much clout. Self-pity just reminds me of a fly caught on a fly-hanger. It makes a pitiful noise, but you can't pity it 'cause you don't like flies. Nobody liked me much, anymore, either.

So, we decided I will teach and Gid has to stop saying I'm not allowed to when I get grouchy. And I have to stop being grouchy. I told them a person who is learning to give up is kind of pitiful, but no one else agreed.

My "main-pain" is still the same. I think everything has to be done in order and on time at home. Laura does very well, but she is, after all, just turning fifteen. So, as always, I feel better if I can only turn into a *chiter* person.

[NOVEMBER 14, 1995]

A Fat Otis

Otis is gaining weight. I'm so afraid he'll look like Junior's Bobby. *Doddy* Kauffmans have a little dog named Bobby that is so fat he looks like a sausage with eyes and legs. You can easily set a soup plate on his back and it will balance nicely. He's so ugly it's pathetic, but he's the best-loved dog in Franklin County. Junior has a natural love for his weird-looking creatures—hedgehogs, beagles (they're cute, though), emus, and ostriches, but Bobby beats them all.

So I'm visualizing Otis looking like Bobby, 'cause I talked about Bobby so *veesht*! You know how the law of life goes. Talk about someone and it comes home to you so fast that it isn't even funny. Surely Otis won't be quite as homely as Bobby, though. Andy declared up and down he'll get so fat he'll just stand or sit. Oh well, fat wife, fat dog. Isn't that a saying or something?

[NOVEMBER 14, 1995]

Indian or Angel?

Laura had school at Bena Lantz's today, and she usually brings the little girls out to school first, on the scooter, of course. It was so cold today, and I worried about them. They were cold, with teeth chattering and noses red. Tonight Laura said Emily was all covered up sitting in the basket, and suddenly she hollered, "There's that Indian!"—meaning the birdbath with a statue of a cherub on it, which we always pass. It's actually an angel, and it's close to school. Laura said she thinks Emily was so relieved to know they were almost at school. So to a three-year-old, I suppose Indians and angels aren't all that different.

No book work tonight, so we duplicated copies of songs for songbooks. Monday's ironing, supper, and dishes, and it's sweet dreams for us all.

[NOVEMBER 14, 1995]

Birthday Girl

This is birthday month for us. Gid turned 39, Anna is nine, and Laura turned fifteen today.

David Flaud's Ruthie and Steven came over with a red velvet cake that looks like a picture from *Taste of Home*. They also brought a beautiful picture of a lighthouse, which they bought in North Carolina. It almost brought tears to my eyes to watch Laura unwrap it, and see the pure delight between the two friends. The only shadow for them is that Ruthie turns sixteen in a few weeks, so that means each one will be going their separate ways. I still believe the bond will remain, because they know everything about each other. Grandpa Kauffmans gave her a ceramic lighthouse of Chincoteague Island that plays a tune and the light goes on and turns. She loves anything from the sea, and just detests artificial flowers and things most girls consider pretty. Seems some people have a knack for finding unique gifts.

[NOVEMBER 19, 1995]

Those English Books

I always have the same question. The English books! I still feel they are pushing the pupils too hard. It would be quite different if we weren't Amish. So, perhaps if I teach another year, I'll do what I feel is best, and be happily independent. I still feel the basic arithmetic, reading, and spelling are the most important—especially reading. Give a child a good book, and if he can learn to enjoy reading, he'll automatically acquire many skills. I find, with my schedule, if I'm not careful, I tend to decrease arithmetic, hurry through reading, and simplify geography because of English and vocabulary.

We're happily falling into a routine here at home. Gid is much more supportive, the children take more responsibility, and I'm not so grouchy. The little girls just love to stay at home with Laura since it's cold. Book work is only two evenings a week now.

[NOVEMBER 19, 1995]

Sweet Revenge

The last week of school my feisty little red-haired girl was teasing another first grader. He swung his lunch box and accidentally knocked her on the head. A large bruise and a torrent of tears followed. Revenge was sweet, because she dried her tears, set her chin, and marched right up and hit him indignantly on the shoulder. I had to reprimand them both.

Maybe half an hour later, during art class, this same little girl brought a brightly colored picture to my desk. "Isn't this nice?" she asked. It was her former enemy's picture. I could have cried at the complete forgiveness, with no hard feelings—everything forgiven. Many times over I marvel at the beauty of children's behavior. They have no guile. I often think how Jesus chose one of His disciples standing under a fig tree. "In him was no guile." Children are so constantly forgiving and don't harbor those ill feelings that we do.

[NOVEMBER 19, 1995]

Hunting Season

Gid and Andy are in Bedford County hunting. They'll be home this evening if they both get their buck today. Gid felt they had an excellent chance, as there was about six inches of snow covering the mountain.

The schoolchildren all had different stories of their dad going hunting, or relatives arriving from Lancaster to go hunting. Dan Stoltzfuses live close to the Blue Mountain, and Miriam said they heard five or six shots early in the morning.

[NOVEMBER 27, 1995]

School Blahs

We're practicing for our Christmas program. I must admit, it all looks overwhelming to me. I suppose when I taught school as a teenager I had that youthful optimism and positive attitude, because I can't remember ever feeling quite as helpless. I believe we all grow more cautious as we grow older, having experienced more than teenagers. Oh well, it'll all work out, one way or another. This morning I overslept. Gid was hunting, and Eva and Ruthie were at Mom's today. All of a sudden I didn't feel like playing anymore.

Who felt like scootering through the mud, starting a fire in that cold, old schoolhouse? Everything turned me off. The art on the wall is changing from autumn to a few snowmen and candy canes, and I simply felt like quitting, which is very normal with any one of us who has a job. There are days when you feel so "BLAH!" I start a roaring fire, write arithmetic assignments on the board, the huge front door opens, and John Fisher's boys walk in, noses red from the cold, their hats pushed way down over their ears, and suddenly everything makes sense again. And yes, I had a good day.

[NOVEMBER 27, 1995]

Dust, Go to Sleep

Mrs. Jacob Lapp, thank you, thank you, thank you for your informative letter! You sound like a person I should be. I plan on writing a long letter to you in the near future. My mom and sisters all had a good laugh when I told them you sent me the poem about "Dust, go to sleep, I'm rocking my baby," etc. That has always been a joke among us. How thoroughly I dislike it. I could never happily rock a baby in a messy house. First I cleaned up, then I rocked my baby. But I'm learning, I'm learning.

Laura's housekeeping is much improved. She actually washes slower and more particularly than I do, because she has more patience. Andy's socks are even white.

[NOVEMBER 27, 1995]

Back to School We Go

Slipping and Sliding to School

Snow, sleet, rain, ice, wind, and mud! Just a mixture of everything winter brings. We started for school at 7:00 this morning, and it's a good thing we did because we walked most of the way, pushing our scooters through all of the above.

While trudging up the hills, slipping and sliding down, I began to question this whole thing of teaching school. Since winter has set in, it sure tests everything I ever liked about it. But always, once I'm at school, with the fire started and the pupils present, I enjoy it.

After the long vacations of Christmas and New Year's, it was hard to go back. After sewing, and enjoying the warmth of our cozy house in the morning, I realized more fully how I used to have it. But then, life was so boring.

[JANUARY 3, 1996]

The Gift of Hospitality

On Sunday afternoon we drove Charlie about fourteen miles to David Bylers. David fell and broke his foot at work, so we decided to pay them a visit.

Poor Charlie! He probably wonders what's wrong with us. He tried to turn in at David Flauds, Ben Kurtzes, and Ike Kings, with no luck.

Anyway, Emma made a delicious ham supper, beating the potatoes with her air mixer. Yum! We were so glad we went. I told Gid on the way home that they made us feel so comfortable and at home. I wonder if people feel that way at our house. I sure think that is a gift, to make people feel at home like that.

[JANUARY 3, 1996]

New Year's Day

On New Year's Day I made five dresses and washed a huge laundry. Oh, it was so much fun! Laura usually does all of it, and I thought it was a treat to wash and sew.

In the evening Emanuels and Dad Bylers came for supper. Rhoda made a chicken and rice casserole, and we added steamed carrots, fruit, and fudge-nut bars. Those little twins sure don't look like the premature babies they were! They're starting to gurgle and express themselves in different ways, sitting by themselves and eating cereal and vegetables.

Dad Kauffmans had a singing for the church people who weren't invited at Sam Kings.

We didn't go, so I haven't heard if there was a good turnout. Mom was planning on having hot dogs and sauerkraut, and of course, plenty of other good stuff.

Did everyone eat their pork and sauerkraut on New Year's? I often wonder where that tradition started. I love sauerkraut and mashed potatoes, and if you don't add butter to the potatoes, it's virtually fat free.

[JANUARY 3, 1996]

Otis of Otterbein

Otis followed Joe Blank's children to school one day. He thoroughly enjoyed his day with all the children. Maybe we'll have to make him the official school mascot. "Otis of Otterbein." It has a distinctive ring to it, kind of like "Anne of Green Gables" but "doggy"!

He needs an obedience school these days. He's so disobedient, spoiled rotten, and gets away with everything. Anna was sliding on the ice and her glasses fell off. He promptly snapped them up, making dents in the lenses with his teeth. Anna came crying to the door, and there he sat, as pleased as punch, with those glasses in his mouth. Oh, for a BB gun!

And he roams again. He was at Elmers twice, and goes out to Joe Blanks, and all over the place.

[JANUARY 3, 1996]

Horrible Bovine!

Joe Blanks are starting their goat dairy business. They're laying blocks for the barn, and have around 100 goats already. It sounds like an interesting occupation, and I wish them the very best. Probably goats and I would get along better than cows and I.

I have never fully forgiven the bovine animals. When we had cows at home, I detested them. Getting up to milk in the morning hung a dark cloud over my entire existence. I am not a morning person, and certainly not a cow morning person.

Anyway, this cow mistook my mop of uncombed hair sticking out of my scarf for hay, and wrapped a horrible tongue around it and tugged. I was so mad that I hit her hipbone with my fist, and hurt my fist worse than the hair-pulling. I think I wished mastitis on her for the rest of her life! So, it's very good we are not all alike. Hundreds of women who are better wives than I enjoy their dairy herds and are a great help to their husbands.

[JANUARY 3, 1996]

Visiting Day

Melting, dirty snowbanks, mud, overcast skies, and drizzle.

Well, fellow pilgrims, are we ready for spring? This weather reminds me of life here on earth. Some days are so...well...blah, that you think spring will never come. But it always does, just as our Lord's mercies are sure.

. . . . .

On Thursday the school board members and teachers of Franklin County visited schools in Perry County. We stopped at Amos Stoltzfus's Country Card Shop and what a good place for teachers!

Little prizes for ten or twenty cents, books, cards—you name it, and he has it. Very worthwhile!

We visited four schools, but had to miss one, much to our disappointment.

Now, all school board members everywhere, if you really want to put fresh interest into your schools, take the teachers and go visit other districts' schools. It just does something for you.

Different ideas and methods of teaching can be so very inspiring. When I got home, I just felt like teaching for the rest of my life.

I do admit, after New Year's, I had a struggle not to wish I could just stay home and relax.

Sometimes I wish I could just wash, sew, type, and sleep on the recliner when I feel like it.

After coming home from Perry County, I was all excited about going back to school.

[JANUARY 23, 1996]

Please, Please, Please...

Today we had planned to go skating after dinner, but with rain in the forecast, it was, "Let's go this morning!" Jump up and down, beg, whine, please, please, please. So...alright, we had devotions, everyone bundled up, grabbed their lunches, and...whoops! A van load of company.

I called the boys back, and their shoulders drooped dejectedly as they resigned themselves to their fate!

Fortunately for them, the board members of Dauphin County knew how it felt to be thirteen and on your way to play hockey, because they said they'd visit the other schools first and come back in the afternoon.

So we skated until lunchtime, and had the Dauphin County teachers and board members this afternoon.

We enjoyed having them, as we always enjoy company. Although I always feel like an amateur compared with those professionals, like Linda Speicher who has taught for six years.

But I'm all "into" my teaching again, and the days just fly past.

[JANUARY 23, 1996]

Baby-Sitting

The driver who hauls the schoolchildren asked Laura to baby-sit their eighteen-month-old granddaughter.

She's a little doll, and Laura, Rosanne, and Emily just adore her. I'm hoping it won't prove to be too boring for Laura, as she really doesn't have that much to do right now.

When I get home from school, she's soon out the door, skating or sledding. And she deserves that, after being cooped up with three little girls all day.

[JANUARY 23, 1996]

Skating

The heavy rains on Friday brought lots of flooding, with creeks swelling into fields, scattering ice everywhere. Many fields are flooded, and frozen solid after a few nights of close to zero degrees.

So everyone is skating, skating, and skating.

On Sunday afternoon even Otis and Emily went along. We took hot chocolate, cookies, and cheese curls, plus a blanket to sit on. Old Otis was in his glory, sitting right beside us, smiling, and gobbling up the cheese curls.

Rosanne is learning to skate, and she took a couple of nasty tumbles. Oh, she held her head and just cried and cried. But that's the only way to learn—just get out there and do it.

Anna is just an exact picture of me when I was nine years old. Little and round and she flies along, turning on a dime. And when she falls, she just bounces and rolls and sits there, grinning so silly. What is more the epitome of youth than a smooth pond, a pair of skates, hot chocolate, and plenty to eat?

[JANUARY 23, 1996]

Welcome Surprises

On Tuesday Mosie Lantz brought a note to school, saying someone will be at Ben Lantzes at 4:00 that would like to meet me. We had come with a driver that day, and I asked if he minds stopping at Bens a few minutes. There were Gid, Laura, and the little girls, all dressed up, and Bena had a surprise supper for all of us! I was taken totally by surprise, and it all worked perfectly for everyone. That sure made my day.

Sometimes I just don't feel worthy of all the kindness and support. Only other teachers will know how much it means to have a child come to your desk with an encouraging note, or a sticky bun wrapped in aluminum foil to put on the stove, or a little gesture which says, "I care."

These winter days can get long and dull, and I think the children become more argumentative and mischievous. But when you think of 33 children together in one schoolhouse all day, it's surprising we don't have more to straighten out.

[JANUARY 29, 1996]

...Another's Good Fortune

Skating is the greatest thing for nine upper grade boys, as they play some fierce games of hockey. Competition is tough, and Friday they were just wild to go skating at 12:00. I told them we will have English, spelling test, our poems, and an art project, then they may go.

When they all finally exploded out the back door with their sticks and skates, I breathed a silent sigh of relief.

John King's Alvin, a second grader, was so excited that he could hardly speak, trying to tell me about his new hockey skates. Sure enough, he had a good pair of skates, and he skated across the pond like a pro, eyes shining and a big grin across his face! Everyone was so excited for him, and the first grade boys ran up to ask if I'm watching Alvin. I was so touched by their generosity of spirit.

No one was jealous, or making envious remarks. They just loved Alvin's new skates!

That same day, my daily little notes on my dresser said, "Special is the man who delights in another's good fortune." And I am always astonished at how far ahead of many adults is the sweetness of a child.

[JANUARY 29, 1996]

The Boss

On Wednesday Arie Stoltzfus brought her whole school to visit ours! What a happy surprise for the pupils! They also visited *Mommy* Eva Kauffman, Lydia Hostetler, and *Doddy* Sam Z. Bylers, to sing for them.

Today the Franklin County school board paid us a visit. Now that's nerve wracking, when the boss comes to visit! I always feel like a real amateur, but, oh well, I did my best to act like a professional. And, of course, we were having English. Sometimes I worry about my outspoken opinion of the School-Aid English books. Whose feelings have I hurt? Hopefully, no one's. The longer I teach, the more I can appreciate them, although I still feel a huge advantage is to have them starting at first grade. I have pupils who were introduced to them at third, fourth, and eighth grade, and it's a hard task.

I've come to the peaceful conclusion that we'll do what the pupils are capable of, and if we don't get through the entire book, so be it. We have other subjects that are important, too.

[JANUARY 29, 1996]

Wounded Ego

The home front is going quite smoothly. Laura is very content to stay home with the girls and keep her little Kendall. She shook her head more than once, and announced she's glad she's not me.

When the weather was particularly wild, she appreciated her warm, cozy home. I know someday my job will be taken, as she takes an avid interest in teaching.

My ego stays very low through Becky and Anna's forthright remarks. They say they'd rather go to Stoney Creek, to Marianne Zimmerman, 'cause she's a better teacher. So much for feeling like a good teacher! Andy never says much. He just goes to school on Beauty, the horse Amos Blanks let him ride. He flies through his lessons (and gets hardly anything right), so he can draw. He is not a student, that's for sure, and it doesn't bother him at all.

I think I'm improving as a morning person. Before I taught school, I opened one eye, threw on a housecoat and made breakfast for Gid without comment. I hated to be civil in the morning. Now I get up at 5:15, fry mush and eggs, and pack five lunch boxes while we keep up a lively conversation. I just thought about that this morning, when Gid looked at me quite admiringly.

He is definitely a morning person, up at 4:30, chirping away all morning, while I used to be less than thrilling. Oh well, there's hope for all of us, even if change seems impossible.

[JANUARY 29, 1996]

Frozen Through

Our thermometer showed -10 this morning. So we let Becky and Anna go with the driver, and Andy and I scootered early. It doesn't seem believable, but we weren't cold. My face hurt and Andy claimed he froze his chin.

Getting to school is no problem, but it was a bit chilly until we had that huge coal stove cleaned out and a roaring fire started. It was red hot most of the day, and I was never truly warm. Old buildings just aren't insulated like new ones.

I often think of Laura Ingalls when she taught school at the Brewsters when she was a young lady. Probably that little shack she taught in was much colder. They had to be a lot more hardy than us cream puffs, 'cause she used to sweep the dirt down through the cracks in the floor. Gives me another batch of goose pimples to think about it.

[FEBRUARY 5, 1996]

Of Daughters and Pounds

On Saturday afternoon, Verna Stoltzfus and I, with all our children, paid Lucy Zimmerman a call. We all have a common bond, being the mothers of four, five, and six girls, along with one boy. Emily, Marilyn, and Rosanna were all born in the summer of '92.

We had an enjoyable day, settled cozily in Lucy's living room with hand sewing, chomping on filled doughnuts and drinking iced tea, lamenting about our weight between bites! Isn't that a fright?

Lucy showed me an article in a magazine that was extremely comforting, about larger ladies who exercise, feel good, and accept their size. Very inspiring, especially when Lucy makes doughnuts.

The kitchen was alive with girls, fifteen of them. They all had fun, skating and having a snack. Laura and Lisa are both fifteen and don't consider themselves little anymore!

[FEBRUARY 5, 1996]

Mysteries and Visitors

I just finished baking a double batch of whoopie pies, while the girls fixed a salad. We're having a mystery dinner at school tomorrow, and it's been a hectic evening. Yummasetti, hot dogs, and finger Jell-O will be part of our menu, and we'll play games in the afternoon.

Uncle Ben Stoltsfuses and their school board members and teachers were our visitors bright and early this morning. Ike and Sarah King joined us, too. Later in the day the Juniata school board and their teachers paid us a visit, which brought many memories of my days at Black Rock. Ben and Barbie Esh brought a delicious lasagna dinner, and a group of girls from Perry County and Franklin visited this afternoon.

Through all the visitors, we kept up all our schedule and the boys claim, "It isn't *chite* how many visitors we get!" But their eyes are shining, and I know they're proud of all the attention we're receiving.

Thanks to all of you for coming. We appreciated you and enjoyed the day. We are especially grateful to the parents. You will never fully realize how much the support and understanding you give makes a teacher feel appreciated. It makes everything worthwhile and puts a song of joy in your heart the rest of the day.

[FEBRUARY 13, 1996]

Dad Kauffman

Dad Kauffman is not well. We are all saddened to see him losing the capability of handling different situations. His head has a constant buzzing, and it feels much like his legs. He falls asleep instantly, wherever he is, and just seems withdrawn and quiet.

Sometimes I feel so sorry for him that I can hardly bear it. He's had a long siege of M.S., and when we see him losing out, it hurts so much. But we strive to keep our eyes on the part we cannot see, where his poor legs may be strong again.

[FEBRUARY 13, 1996]

Butchering

Gid, Laura, Andy, and Becky helped butcher five pigs at Brother Emanuels on Saturday.

I know how ignorant I am, but I refused to help. Gid just shrugged his shoulders, and was greatly relieved to let me stay out of it. Raw meat and butchering is like a huge mountain to me. In plain words, I don't like to butcher.

I never "took out" a chicken. I mean, I never took a chicken out. Somehow, that isn't worded right. It seems like I would have been sitting in a restaurant with a chicken, having a nice lunch. I never took the…ahem…how do you say it? intestines, liver, etc., out of a chicken.

Anyway, all week Gid and the three oldest were bragging about butchering. "What's wrong with you, Mom?"

Well, now Laura and Becky know. They were less than thrilled by the time the day was over. But Gid enjoyed it fully, and the scrapple and sausage are delicious.

[FEBRUARY 13, 1996]

Precious Memories

David Lapps of Michigan, my sister Mary, and their family were at Dads the day we butchered. So that was my main excuse. Mom invited Debbie Sigler from Juniata to surprise Mary, and it was a happy surprise. We talked of our childhood, how we roamed the ridges, slept in the haymow, and went skating, picnicking, and swimming. There were so many memories that it brought tears to our eyes. Wayne Troyer Verna, all we needed to complete the day was you! The green cupboard and your mom's cookies and chopped ham sandwiches. Food was always a part of our life.

We talked of having a reunion for the children who played cowboys and Indians on the ridge.

[FEBRUARY 13, 1996]

Grouchy Brother

Otis is tired of winter. He's an old grouch. He barked at Mom Byler when she came over to borrow something, and he prowls around on the porch like an old bear.

Andy claimed tonight he just likes him better than ever. "He's my brother," he claimed, and a funny-looking brother I'd say. But they're inseparable in the evening.

. . . . .

The kitchen is filled with little girls' giggles. Dan Stoltzfus's Miriam is here overnight, and they're having a wonderful time. Anna and Miriam are both in third grade and the best of friends.

[FEBRUARY 13, 1996]

Losing It

Spring! Tons of mud, and this teacher just about "lost it." Snow, ice, rain, and cold weather did not bother me like the sticky mud. Sweeping the schoolhouse was much like a farmer cleaning his forebay. We opened all the windows and the brown dust swirled over everything. A load of gravel helped a lot and Friday evening we thoroughly cleaned. We put the brooms, rugs, dustpans, and everything under the pump and doused them with pine cleaner.

Fresh art on the windows, violets and kites, along with a clean schoolroom, lifted my spirits considerably.

[FEBRUARY 27, 1996]

Screaming and Kicking

Friday evening we had surprise overnight guests. Priscilla Glick and her boys, who were on their way to Lancaster to visit her parents, stopped for the night on account of a sleepy driver. She was a stranger when she came, but felt like an old friend when she left. These hardy women who move so far away from familiar surroundings and loved ones, leave me in awe. They truly do have that, "Whither thou goest, I will go" love for their husbands. Well, I would too; after I got done screaming and kicking, and the dust would settle, I believe I would go with Gid. First would come a royal battle, though!

[FEBRUARY 27, 1996]

This Little Fatty

Saturday we cleaned, baked cake and brownies, and scootered to Dad Kauffmans. Dad was a bit better, although I had to talk slowly and clearly so he could follow. Gid came over in the evening, and Stephen Lees and Aaron Eshes also paid them a visit.

Sunday morning we were invited to Amos Eshes for breakfast. Stephen Lees, Jr. Eshes, Benuel Blanks, and us. Casseroles, French toast, ham, eggs, coffee cake, and shoofly; yum-yum. We had a tour of three new places, and it was all very interesting.

David Bylers were our supper guests, and I made fried chicken for David, as he claims he looks forward to it. Dad Bylers joined us, too.

Now this little fatty is on a diet. After my delicious breakfast and fried chicken for supper I weighed in at my limit on Monday morning! I was so disgusted. So I drank water with vinegar in it this week, and greatly reduced my fat intake. Already I feel better. Vinegar water helps me when I retain fluid and feel especially fat and ugly.

[FEBRUARY 27, 1996]

Too Many Cats

The most dreadful thing happened last night. Andy shot one of Becky's cats. It wasn't even funny. Becky came crying in despair, followed by Anna, lamenting loud and long, tears running down their faces.

We do need to get rid of some cats, and it's been a subject of controversy in our family. That is only a nice way to say we spent many suppers arguing loud and long over the fate of Becky's cats! She has seven, and we go through one bag of cat food after another. And I've often stressed that it's more humane to shoot them than send them with Bruce Rotz, the kennel man.

To make a long story short, Andy decided the time is here to get rid of them, and took matters in his own hands. What a battle! They have never fully forgiven each other; the feud has simmered since Otis was a puppy, and it was like a volcano erupting last evening.

We settled it all by allowing two cats, and that's it. So it remains to be seen what will happen to the remaining six, and whether Becky will hang Otis or not! I'm sure revenge would be sweet.

She'll give up and things will all settle down. After all, Andy has only one dog, and a family member he is. Laura is not a dog lover, and she even claimed he's probably one of those dogs we'll keep until he dies, then everyone will cry. I don't know if he stirs my emotions or not.

[FEBRUARY 27, 1996]

Broken and Helpless

Another day that the Lord hath made, enabling Dad to see another light of day.

He took a turn for the worse Thursday evening, and Friday all we children and grandchildren were summoned to his bedside.

It all seems inadequate to try and express feelings on paper at such a time. He is totally broken, helpless in body, and yet so alive in spirit, with his mind bright and alert. Oxygen relieved his labored breathing, and he cried and pleaded and admonished us all. He asked to be anointed, and Christ Esh and Israel administered this for him. He became stronger after this, and we went home to our duties and to church services at Levi and Mamie Kings on Sunday.

After church we all gathered at Dad's bedside again, and they called the five families who live in other states, our brothers and sisters.

He kept talking, but weakly, and seemed to be waiting on Leroy, my brother from North Carolina.

Many touching incidents, and we stayed till 12:30. It seemed he slept deeply and peacefully after Leroys came, and we came home and I'm back at school today, with mixed emotions. I know Dad longs for heaven, and all will be well, but how does one part bravely with a parent?

Mose Hostetlers were here this morning, with a roaring fire started, and Sarah had just finished cleaning the floor! What a wonderful thing to do. I was tired, but still felt life goes on, and there are duties that must be done. I trust Mom to send for me if he gets lower.

A little girl was born, and Dad is lying near death's door. Such is the process of life, and all in God's order. From dust we are made, and to dust we return, and our faith and love to Jesus Christ and our fellow men is all that counts in between.

Surely He is a merciful Father.

[MARCH 4, 1996]

History of Otterbein

I will include Sally Flaus's history of this Otterbein schoolhouse. She said I may change it, but she did just fine.

It is a touching story and adds lots of meaning to these loose windows.

Thank you, Sally, for sharing with us.

"In 1971, when Franklin County started, we noticed the old Otterbein schoolhouse on the Charles Brenize farm. This farm joins Ben Lantzes. Some of the men went to ask Charles if we could buy or rent the schoolhouse. He said it was used for a school, later on the Boy Scouts and then the Otterbein church youth used it. He said their fences would get torn down and they really didn't take care of the building, and that they like it better if it's not being used. The Amish built another school. About three years later we needed another school. This schoolhouse was still standing there empty. They decided to try again, but to no avail.

In 1974, Charles's brother Art's barn burned down. This had been the old Brenize homestead. They asked if our people could build an old-fashioned barn, mortised and pinned together, that would look like the old one that was there before. The men living in the area helped to get it ready. Then on February 5, 1974, a very cold day, three bus loads from Lancaster County came out to help the day of the raising, and it was almost completed that day. That evening as we were milking, Charles came to the barn with tears in his eyes and said he wants the Amish to use the Otterbein schoolhouse. We have now been using it for 22 years. We still want to thank everyone who helped. With not more families that were in the area at the time, we would not have gotten very far without the help of our Lancaster County friends. This is the school where Linda Byler now teaches. Charles and Art both died this last year. Both widows are still living on their farms. Charles died of heart problems, and Art had leukemia."

[MARCH 4, 1996]

Windy School Sale

The annual school sale was held on Saturday. Showers in the morning and humid weather turned into a severe thunderstorm in the afternoon. Hundreds of people sought shelter under the sturdy pole shed, although some men were drenched trying to keep the large tent anchored to the ground.

Amos Stoltzfus had some things lost, and Gid Fisher's ice cream tent blew away, but all in all, the damage was hardly noticeable.

I decided it takes a generous heart to host that school sale. All those people, and the work involved, takes a commitment from some caring people. I think everyone, especially Jake and Daniel Flauds, need a hearty round of applause.

The lunch stand is a well-managed

affair, thanks to the school board members. Stephen Lee was all sold out of his barbecued chicken soon after lunch and I missed out on it.

[MAY 13, 1996]

School Gives Way to Summer

Laura just came home from work at Elmer's greenhouse with a huge geranium in a planter for the patio—my Mother's Day gift. Homemade cards, and a "real" one. Sorry we're late, Mom, but it all means the same.

. . . . .

These past weeks have been a little crazy with all these final tests to check and report cards to do. I have divided so many numbers by six that I declare I dreamed of dividing things one night. We had a few tense evenings, hunched over the kitchen table, resulting in a headache and stiff neck that would not go away. Excedrin did the trick for the headache though. I need glasses and am too contrary to admit it.

Tomorrow is the picnic! I'm glad school is over. The past month has been trying, with work at home, and everyone has lost all enthusiasm for school.

Sometimes I ask myself what I have accomplished. After finals, I felt like a total failure. What have they learned? And you think of all the subjects you should have stressed more, etc., until it gives you the blues. Was I really supposed to teach this year?

But doubting just makes a restless wreck of yourself, so I keep searching for the positive side.

There is so much good in every situation, and today as the children were cleaning up, with weed eaters whining, horse shed being cleaned, and junk hauled away, I just stood at the door and watched. Some of the poorest students were hard at work, managing, smiling, and looking well adjusted to any situation.

I just felt my feeling of dejection rise, and I realized again that there is more to life than A's on a report card, and each child has his own God-given talent.

Schools are really no different than families or churches—so many shortcomings and failures, and things don't always go the way we think they should, but that is where love comes in.

As long as we honestly love the children, so much good can come of it. Forgiving, forgetting, sharing, admonishing, and helping them along as best as we can.

And that is the whole meaning of life. I suppose the straight and narrow; when in truth, you could just spank those mischievous boys and shake those slow ones till their teeth rattle. And send Andy home and let his dad deal with him. But on we go, and now the year is at an end. What a relaxing summer is ahead for me—yard sales, sisters' days, iced tea, and the flyswatter!

. . . . .

Will I teach again? I doubt if they'll ask me. Honestly.

[MAY 13, 1996]

Father's Day

We had a surprise when Ike Kings came for breakfast. Although we were second choice, we really enjoyed them, even if our breakfast was simple. They were on their way to Joe Blanks when they met them going through Mowersville on their way to church at Stevie Smokers.

We had late lunch at Dan Kauffmans then, where Israels, Jimmys, and Amoses were, too. Mom had hot dogs and sauerkraut, hamburgers, refreshing salads, and desserts. She made Dad's favorite things for Father's Day, and he got cards and a book. He tried to tell us how unworthy he is, but just choked up. Dear Dad, and these warm summer days he just has to give up and accept how weak he becomes at day's end.

[JUNE 17, 1996]

Who Wants a Cow?

Grandma Kauffman gave Laura a butter churn that was her mother's. A nice gesture, as Laura likes old things, antiques or whatever.

Well, this Gid had been bugging me for a year or more to get a cow to make our own cheese and butter, cottage cheese, yogurt, etc.; now this really got him started. He sat on the recliner with a blissful expression, turning the handle and insisting we get a cow. Oh dear, I don't want to get a cow. I like my 2% milk, cold and fresh out of the refrigerator, no slop, no dirty tail in my face, no milking, no straining with flies buzzing all over you and the milk. I just kind of stayed quiet, and let him ramble on about buying only sugar, flour, and salt at the grocery store. He thinks it would be so neat to live like they used to. But look out if he wants a glass of iced tea or a dish of Wheaties or a couple pretzels and cheese. The cow is on "hold" for now.

[JUNE 17, 1996]

Soothing Cinnamon Rolls

We had fresh peas and strawberry shortcake tonight. Peas are a bountiful crop this year, but strawberries are not doing as well for us.

. . . . .

I found a recipe for cinnamon rolls in the Canada Amish cookbook that Dannie King sei Susie gave me when I taught school as a teenager. Gid just loved them! Can you imagine? He ate three with a cup of coffee and pronounced them the best I ever made.

How soothing that was to my battered ego. Truthfully, they were hard, too.

[JUNE 17, 1996]

Caught a... Boy!

As I sit here, my conscience pricks me terribly. I made a chocolate cake for Lydia, and in the confusion of the morning it stayed here, and never did get up to Elmers.

Andy was running up the stairs to get ready to go to church, carrying a lure that was lying on the desk—an artificial minnow with a hook on each end. He caught one end in his pants, which pulled the other end into his finger. He went to the shop and tried to pull it out with a pliers, but he couldn't. There was nothing to do but go to the emergency room and watch attentively and with interest as the doctor numbed it and cut and removed the hook, with blood flowing over everything. I kind of hummed and read something on the wall. It was all very efficient, and we returned to church while they were still singing.

[JUNE 23, 1996]

McClays Mills

This week the excavator was busy in the field where the new school will be built. The footer was poured, and they laid the blocks yesterday. It all amounts to some high excitement at our house. I thought Anna would pop a blood vessel from hollering when the concrete truck went past. Gid, Benuel Blank, and Jr. Esh are on the building committee, so we will have a busy dad this summer. That's okay. My water pipe is fixed in the wash house, and the rest of the "honey-dos" are not that important.

The school meeting was held at Stevie Smokers on Tuesday evening. David Flaud's Ruthie has consented to teach at Sunset and Eva Lantz at Otterbein. Our new school will be named "McClays Mills," which I think sounds so neat. I'm not sure if that is spelled right or not, but I don't feel like running out to the end of South Road to look.

[JUNE 23, 1996]

Sewing...Oh, Groan!

It's Mollie time again, meaning little Mollie Van Lieu is spending a week with Becky. My, how they look forward to this time when school lets out! They are trying to persuade me to go camping this week, but we are too busy, with the frolic at the school on Saturday, and my sewing. Oh, groan. I have so much sewing to do. Not too much got done during the winter, and after sewing again, I realize how much I do like it.

[JUNE 23, 1996]

Perfect Timing

Eva had buddies' day again, and I was a bit late as my driver didn't come on time. These poor ladies were out in the rain, picking peas as fast as they could, and unfortunately, I made a grand entrance just as they finished. How lucky can you get? They weren't too impressed, and claimed they wish they would have stopped early and got me out of bed. Too bad.

[JUNE 23, 1996]

Ring, Ring, Ring...

I bought a little toy telephone for Emily. I think she must have the greatest imagination for a child her age. I was working outside and she went puffing past, all out of breath, lamenting to herself, and I asked her what's wrong. She said she just can't understand why her phone rings all the time. She hurried in, and I followed her, just to watch. She picked up the receiver, and in a very grown-up voice, speaking English, she said, "Hello!" After a pause, she said, "Of course not. I went to Wal-Mart today, and they should stop calling so often."

[JUNE 23, 1996]

Many Churches, One Community

It's not very often that I am on the road on a Sunday morning, going to Chambersburg. It was really fascinating to see all the different churches, and the members arriving around 9:00. First we passed Elmers, where all the teams were parked, and then Air Hill, where a large congregation was arriving, then past Culberston Mennonite. I had to wonder at the different cultures and churches, yet we all worship the same God. Probably each church had their failures and mistakes, and we would not all agree with what each preacher said. Or would we?

In Revelation there were seven different churches, and most of them failed in some way. We all do. But that is where we must come in faith and believe in the grace of our Lord. On that subject, I'm sure all those churches would be united. It all seemed so simple and so beautiful, what the whole meaning of life actually is. We don't have to know who is right and who is wrong; that's not our job.

. . . . .

Well, it's not my job to ramble on about this subject either, so I will close. Gid is making steaks on the grill, and I will muster all my willpower and not eat any. Or not very much. Maybe just a little. Ben Bylers, Dad Bylers, and Emanuels were here for supper last evening, and I ate too much. It was so relaxing, visiting and eating, that time just flew, and so did the food! *Ach*, my.

[JUNE 23, 1996]

Many Hands Make Light Work

Foggy morning, thunderstorms, hot and humid, just typical July weather. Wonderful growing weather, and the gardens look nice.

There is a schoolhouse in the hay field across the road since Saturday. A group of men and boys made short work of erecting the neatest little schoolhouse. I am so excited, but trying hard to act casual, as a grown-up mother should. If I'd do as I felt, I'm afraid it would be one unladylike whoop.

Maryann Blank and Becca Esh furnished coffee break in the forenoon, and everyone ate dinner here. It was all so exciting, as we watched this school being built. Gid said it was the best frolic he has ever attended, with the work going smoothly and done right. Thank you, everyone, for helping. Also, thanks to the busy mother who baked a cake at 10:00 Friday evening.

[JULY 1, 1996]

Sunburned Mollie

Mollie, our little boarder, went swimming with the children two days in a row, and being very fair, she burned so badly that a doctor's visit was required. She did not want me to call her mother, as she was afraid she would come to get her. Of course, I had to contact her, but assured her she was getting the best care available. Becky was Mollie's faithful nurse and companion through all her misery. Great big water-filled blisters swelled off her shoulders, and the doctor said it is actually a second-degree burn. Silvadene cream brought her instant relief, and the poor child could finally sleep. She slept with Laura the night before, and actually woke Laura with her shivering and fever. She also was sick to her stomach. I never knew anyone could get so burned from the sun. Our children are all darker complected, and only use sun lotion 'cause it smells so good. She persuaded her mother last evening when they came to get her, that it really isn't fair, the sunburn ruined her vacation, and would she be allowed to spend another week? Upon receiving her mother's okay, she smacked Becky and let out a genuine yell of joy. So we have her till Saturday afternoon.

[JULY 1, 1996]

On Her Own

I felt like crying this morning when Laura left at 7:00 with David Flauds to go to Lancaster, where Davids are attending the "Hump" reunion, and Laura and Ruthie will spend three days with Aaron Esh's Sylvia. She was so excited, and I was glad she could go, but, oh dear, I feel so lost without her. So I did not go back to bed. I washed early, and cut six pairs of pants for Andy, and pedaled all day, stopping only to fold and put away the wash. I cleaned flower beds tonight, and feel very capable of being on my own.

We decided on Friday that we don't get any more done together than I do alone. We sit on the couch and eat licorice, talk, and just plain goof off when we're cleaning. Becky doesn't have to do very much when Mollie's here, and feels extremely privileged.

[JULY 1, 1996]

Sic 'em!

Andy devised a new way of producing scooter power. He took hold of Otis's collar and yelled, "Sic 'em!" which is like putting gunpowder under Otis. He took off like a rocket and Andy hung on, having a free ride in from the school. Otis was puffing, and his tongue hung way out from the collar being too tight. Poor Otis, he is faithful beyond all reason. Such obedience to his master almost breaks your heart. I'm sure he was not comfortable, and yet, if Andy says, "Sic 'em," that is exactly what he will do.

Our scooters were all battered and well worn after their school year at Otterbein. Finally it got so bad that we had only one scooter that didn't have a flat tire or needed the basket replaced. Today Gid spent some time fixing them, and I am so grateful. What did we ever do without them?

[JULY 1, 1996]

My Little Baker

I think, after all these years, I have a little baker! Anna, who is nine years old, and chubby, asked if she could bake cookies last week. Why, of course. And she made chocolate chip cookies, with only a little advice from me. This morning she asked again, and made "cow patties," and are they ever delicious! I praised her highly, knowing that would only add to her interest in baking. She flies around the kitchen, humming under her breath, squinting carefully over her measuring cups to make sure she has the proper amount, and I really do believe she enjoys it. Needless to say, Laura and Becky also praise her as much as they can.

[JULY 1, 1996]

More of the Same

Sigh. Tomorrow will be more of the same. Sew. ARRRRGH. But I will not make a fuss, just cut and sew determinedly all day. *Mommy* Lydia Byler just nodded her head, and could really identify with my after-school depression. She says it's because your overloaded days are suddenly empty, and you do go through something. Whew. It's a relief to know I'm not as abnormal as I thought. What is more dear to one teacher than another one who knows what you mean? So many teacher friends, and they had teachers' class in Perry today. My heart was there, but my place is at home, with no Laura, and Mollie and little Kendall to take care of.

Well, this whole letter is about only us again. Oh dear. I know there were Indiana visitors in the area, but have no idea who they were, or where they went. That's not very newsy. It's getting dark and I'm getting a wart on my little finger. Must be the toad that was trapped in the phone shanty.

[JULY 1, 1996]

Paintin' and Gabbin'

Rain, rain, rain. The little raindrops are dancing on the patio, as I sit here at my desk.

It does feel good to sit down and relax after painting the interior walls of the school today. Benuel Blank sei Anna, Jr. Esh sei Rebecca, Laura, and I tackled the job. It was fun, with our mouths going right along with the roller. Becky was the baby-sitter and she had a real little troop of well-behaved children.

[JULY 30, 1996]

Another Surgery

I just talked to Mom and she said Dad has a stone the size of a walnut in his bladder. They have been having problems with the catheter, so he was taken to the doctor. Now he will have to undergo surgery, and Mom is afraid the doctors don't realize how very weak he is. I could tell how much she dreads the surgery, but is trying to leave it all in God's hands. Sometimes I marvel how she is given the strength to go on, with her sleepless times at night while Dad is restless or uncomfortable. Only other people who take care of an invalid can truthfully feel for Mom. They need our prayer support.

[JULY 30, 1996]

Accident-Prone Andy

Andy's "sawdust" turned out to be a piece of steel imbedded in the blue part of his eye. By Monday morning he was in agony, just walking around with tears streaming down his face.

I had to take him to emergency room, because the doctor said if it's that serious he won't take him. So they numbed the eye and, using a small drill, extracted the steel, which the body had already begun to absorb. Nothing to it, and with a smile, Andy hopped off the table, glad it was so easy. We had to get dark glasses for him, and while at the store the numbness wore off and the pain was intense. I really do wonder what people thought, seeing this plain mom with a boy as tall as herself, wearing a wild pair of sunglasses and crying like a baby. Pain in an eye must be severe, because normally he can stand a lot of pain.

Then last week he smashed his finger with the hammer at work. Blood spurted, the nail is black, and the whole finger swelled up terribly. He climbed down and went out to the van, and his good friend Davey Blank trailed him to lend moral support and ask if he's alright. Gid just smiled and shook his head. I think he was kind of proud of the smashed finger. Like this was a manhood ritual of some sort that all true carpenters experience. He promptly launched a whole row of episodes where he smashed his fingers, telling us every gory detail. Andy's eyes were shining as he listened to this, and I do believe he pushed his chest out, as if now he was a true carpenter. He smashed his finger!

[JULY 30, 1996]

Fire!

Our ordinary Sunday turned into an extraordinary one, seeing smoke across the knob where White Oak Mills have three hog units. The girls went to investigate, and ran back with the news that the hog barn was on fire. I called 911 and instantly our quiet little dirt road was transformed. Fire trucks, cars, and people everywhere. Whee. The fire-proof insulation saved the little piggies that were housed in that particular building, but the firemen had a job removing the steel roof to get to the smoldering fire.

[JULY 30, 1996]

Bye-Bye, Kitties

Our cat situation finally came to the breaking point so Becky called a local vet and had a long conversation with him. How much does it cost to put fifteen cats to sleep? She came in and tried to contain her tears as she related her story. The vet suggested shooting them, but she thinks she'll save her money and eventually she'll have $115.00. Poor Becky. I couldn't bear her anxiety, so that evening I raised my eyebrows in the most pitiful manner and implored Gid as nicely as I could to please do something about these cats. And he did. He built a wire cage, and Becky helped round them up, grimly biting her lips to keep from crying. But when her beloved kitties fought, scratching and biting, it was too much. She came in sobbing and sniffing, just heartbroken. So Gid and Andy shot nine of them, while I consoled her, telling her it's just the same as putting them to sleep. It just sounds horrible. *Doddy* shot the one that eats the birds, so now she only has five. Two of them she wants to keep, and they have little collars with bells, and the remaining three will have to be disposed of. Hopefully we have learned our lesson with cats.

[JULY 30, 1996]

Meanest Mom Ever!

Cold, dismal, and rainy. It feels like the kind of day you should throw all cares aside and curl up with a cozy blanket, a good book, and a cup of hot chocolate. And if you're one of those fortunate few who doesn't have to watch their weight, a few whoopie pies would be very nice.

Laura is at Ruthie's place today, helping her do peaches. My day was planned differently, as I wanted to help my friend Lorna Yoder paint their house. They bought a trailer and added a roof and siding, which we want to paint. So I feel a bit relaxed, although I could always sew, make vegetable soup, make posters, lengthen dresses, etc.

Anna and Rosanne are furious. They think I am the meanest mom there ever was, because they were complaining about having nothing to do, so they have to do the dishes and sweep the kitchen while I happily type. I do hear them singing now, so they have accepted their sad fate rather well.

[AUGUST 12, 1996]

Almost Finished

Two more Saturdays till school starts. They have been working steadily, but there is still work to be done. John Petersheim will lay the tile floor, there is still trim work to be done, bricks to be laid, the horse shed and privies are incomplete, there is grass to be sown, and gulp...I never say a word to push things along, as I vowed I would not. We built three houses since we're married, and every time we'd fall out, because I was too impatient. Gid is helping out real well, much better than I would sometimes, and Jr. and Benuel do a good job, considering that both of them are building a barn this summer. So, in two weeks, presumably, I will be a teacher again. My only concern today, with the rain pouring from leaden skies, is how do you keep twenty children off a playground? The grass will not be up.

I'm moaning and groaning in silence; wonder if I should have started to nag.

[AUGUST 12, 1996]

Where Did the Summer Go?

Tomorrow I'm planning on going to Bennie K.'s to work on some quilts. They are having a benefit sale for hospital bills, and I did not go at all to help yet this summer. What happened to the summer? Looking back, it seems like yesterday that I sat on the porch at Otterbein waiting on my driver to take a load of stuff home.

[AUGUST 12, 1996]

Volleyball

Elmer Fishers and their Jason rode by on their scooters yesterday, and they stopped to visit a while. Gid was making steaks on the grill, while the rest of us were playing one long seemingly endless game of volleyball with Lenny, the mildly retarded neighbor boy. Alvin Fishers are having the neighborhood picnic on Friday evening, and Lenny is all excited. He spied our volleyball net from the road, which means he has to practice for the picnic.

The girls do a good job of being kind to him though, and he is kind of fun to have around. Although how long can four people have an exciting game of volleyball? And Lenny never tires of it.

[AUGUST 12, 1996]

Good Morning, Neighborhood

On Saturday I scootered over to Mom to do her Saturday cleaning and yard work. It was interesting to watch the neighborhood wake up. Israels had all gone to Lancaster and that area was quiet. Dad was still in bed, and Mom was canning pickles. Little Leroy came out of the house, and was greeted by his cocker spaniel puppy in the most effusive manner. Leroy was rubbing his ears, and the puppy was ecstatic, with his little stubby tail wagging as fast as possible. It was so cute. A miniature version of Andy and Otis.

. . . . .

Andy is gone so much of the time, and if he stays at work overnight, Otis is in an awful mood. On Friday evening when Andy got home, he was soon out on the porch, just holding Otis by the ears, with his face tight against Otis's, crooning all the while how much he missed him. Pure affection, and Otis was a happy dog again. He's trained to haul Andy on the scooter now. If Andy gets a scooter, and calls Otis, he knows exactly what he wants. Away they go, Otis running full tilt, with Andy hanging on.

. . . . .

Molly is coming again tonight, to stay for a week before school starts. Becky is all excited, and no comment from Laura.

[AUGUST 12, 1996]

A Deep Feeling of Thankfulness

We are having a beautiful fall day, with puffy white clouds and a cold wind blowing. Don't we all just love it?

Our church services were held at Benuel Blanks today. Ivan and Anna Stoltzfus and Benjamin Lantz were baptized and became members of our church. How can mere words express our feelings? We can honestly say, God heard the fervent prayers of the valley, and the sheep have returned to the fold. The Lord is so good, and to Him goes all the honor and praise.

I think the congregation was bound together today in a deep feeling of thanksgiving. I just had to look at all the older members and thank God for these precious pillars of prayer. As the bishop said today, God is still patiently waiting for the other ones who will come later.

[SEPTEMBER 15, 1996]

Rules Are Rules

School is going well, and I am enjoying my days. We had visitors on Friday. Aunt Mamie Lantz had her 56th birthday, and her daughters-in-law surprised her by visiting schools here in Franklin. *Mommy* Kauffman and Bena were along, and we enjoyed their visit. Later in the day, Susie Lee and Jr. sei Rebecca came to visit too.

Talk about a youthful opportunist. Last week when it was so hot, and everyone was sweating when they came in from recess, the children were fanning with paper and books, or whatever they could find. They know when I read a story, they must keep their papers inside their desks. But I was told later that third grader Gideon Blank, who has blond hair, blue eyes, one front tooth sticking out, and freckles—a perfect Tom Sawyer—made a bunch of paper fans, sticking a sign on his desk saying, "Fans for Sale." I am sure he would have been in business if it would not have been for the rules.

[SEPTEMBER 15, 1996]

Oh, to Be an Author

Laura taught on Wednesday and the buddies came to clean upstairs. And did they ever give that old place a polish! Some people like me clean ordinarily, but some clean really well. They were all very thorough, and the furniture was so clean and polished that when I stood on a dresser to replace a blind, I almost fell flat on my face. I told the children, it's straight to bed that night; don't even look right or left, just walk in a straight line and carefully climb into bed. What an accomplishment! I love those buddies, for sure.

Laura thoroughly enjoyed her day at school. She is already getting things ready for next year, and I tell her, "What if the school board would rather have me?" I would never think of taking it away from her, and my real ambition is to become an author, anyway. Is that too ambitious or high minded? I hope not. I have a dream of writing, and hopefully, someday the Lord will guide me in that direction.

[SEPTEMBER 15, 1996]

Back to School for Andy

Andy is alone in eighth grade this year, and would be out of school, but he needed to repeat second grade in the Mennonite school. He will be almost fifteen by the time he's out, and he'll never attend vocational class.

He was asked recently how he feels about this. I think he answered honestly, by saying he would rather be on Amos Blank's carpenter crew, but it isn't that bad being in school. He added that it is no fun going to school when you simply cannot do your lessons.

When he was in second grade, he ruined one shirt after another by chewing on the collars. He was a nervous wreck because he had almost no memory and things were so hard for him. I am still very grateful to his teacher, for caring enough to put him back. When he was told that he would repeat second grade, I asked him if it's just too hard. He promptly burst into tears and said he didn't care to go back, it's just too hard.

Although I realize there are many pros and cons on this subject, I am grateful to parents who cooperate when a child cannot cope with the grade they are in.

Now it is a bit hard to submit to going to school again, but I feel it is good for him, to learn what he can this last year.

Otis goes along to school every day, and has the best life out there. The children love him, and he is fed snacks, and he naps on the rug in front of the door during class. Outside!

[SEPTEMBER 15, 1996]

Runaways

Beautiful September weather. There is so much to report this time that I hardly know where to begin, which seems so different. We had buddies' day at Elmer Fishers, where we all gathered to quilt. She had two in frame, one for Priscilla and an old favorite that had worn through, so she put new batting in and we did some on that one.

Lydia related how Levi King had a runaway with the binder team. I think one of the horses got tangled in some wire that was connected to the electric fence, and this caused the team to panic. Levi felt he was unable to stay on while rounding a curve to the barn, so he leaped to safety. The team came clattering into the barnyard and stopped, just where they were supposed to. It frightened Mamie, hearing this commotion and seeing the team come in like that without a driver. She had planned on sending little Miriam and Johnny out to tell them to come for dinner, but decided against it when she saw they were coming already. I think they all felt grateful for the Lord's care.

. . . . .

Ruthie Flaud also had a scare at school one morning when Jerry Zook's children's horse became uncontrollable after seeing David Esh's Ervin on horseback. I think John Esh's Marlin was actually the one that got the runaway horse stopped, by stepping out and trying to flag him down. It must have been frightening, because Daniel Flaud's Michael said, "Now I know what a dead gallop means."

[SEPTEMBER 22, 1996]

How Much Is 50¢?

Israel Stoltzfuses are remodeling their house, building two rooms upstairs, and adding a wash house and porch. They had a frolic yesterday, and it did look exciting, all these men tearing off the porch roof and knocking things apart. We were preparing dinner in the kitchen when the ceiling started to come down. Eva seemed calm, cool, and collected, although I seriously wonder how long that will last. Being a mother of eleven children can make her a bit absentminded at times. She was saying how their Stephen, who is seven, walked past her with a deeply troubled expression, muttering how he's just going out to ask his dad. Eva kind of jerked awake and said, "What?" "Oh," Stephen explained tiredly, "I asked you if two quarters were fifty cents and you said you didn't know." Poor Eva, as far as I know she's always been able to count two quarters if she wanted a soda out of the soda machine!

[SEPTEMBER 22, 1996]

Teachers' Class

We had a teachers' class at school on Friday afternoon. All the teachers from Dauphin, Perry, and Franklin, plus *Doddy* Byler came. The girls were all there too, and it was an experience for them, too. I always enjoy going if I can, and also enjoy having them at my school. The school board brought a hot supper for us, and I feel they put lots of effort into the delicious supper. Thank you so much for everything.

Rhoda Petersheim was waiting till past 8:00, so we sat out on the porch and visited until her driver came. Emily and

I walked in through the dark, with only the moon for light. I had my hands full, carrying leftover kettles and bowls, so she hung on to my apron and marched beside me in the dark. I kept her spirits up by telling her she is such a wonderful friend, staying with me so I'm not all alone. She burst through the door, into the well-lit kitchen, as if she had been lost for several days and deserved to be welcomed as a hero.

[SEPTEMBER 22, 1996]

Grrrrr!

Laura has been cleaning house last week. I sew whenever I have a chance, but now on Friday I discovered my sewing machine doesn't work. The thread just tears off. Grrrr. So I took off all the parts that I possibly could and oiled everything, changed the needle—same thing. Grrrrr. So I called Lucy Zimmerman, the seamstress, and she said I should make sure my needle is perfectly straight, and to pull it down, just a tiny bit. And that worked! For a little while. Then snap…there we go again. Grrrrrrrrrrr.

Some people say we should just use some other kind of thread, called Metro something or other, but Lucy says she never uses anything but the ordinary Dual Duty, and if the machine does not sew with it, there is something wrong with the machine, not the thread. I plan on trying to fix it yet, but if not, I will have to send it to Hinkletown to have it repaired. I hope I haven't started a controversy here, 'cause a lot of people have Berninas. They are a very good machine, and the man in Hinkletown is the best place to go, I think. But the mighty fall, and Berninas can go berserk, too.

[SEPTEMBER 22, 1996]

Those Ohio Cooks

We attended the wedding at Paul Millers, where their daughter Leanna became Edward Yoder's bride—a really nice, well-managed wedding, in a neat shop, and the food was so good. I will never be able to bake and cook like those Ohio ladies, although you would suppose I would have a trace of culinary skills somewhere, because Mom comes from Ohio.

On Saturday afternoon I decided to make an apple pie. I found a recipe out of the Ohio cookbook, and to make a long story short, the filling had the consistency of gummy bears. It wouldn't thicken right, so I kept adding clear jel, and it was truly horrible. I think you could have thrown it against the wall, and the filling would have remained intact.

Do you suppose there would be a niche in the market for "Apple Pie, Gummy Bear Style"? Poor Gid, he bravely ate a piece, anyway.

[OCTOBER 14, 1996]

The Trip Home

On the way home from the wedding, our driver slid off her seat while making a turn, and we landed in a fairly deep ditch. Mom's head hit the windshield, and she hurt her back. I had bruises on both shins from hitting the seat in front of me. We were taken to the Millersburg hospital, and a driver from Ohio brought us home.

That sure was a helpless feeling, and I longed for my family. I was so happy to be home at 2:30 on Friday morning. We talked and talked and talked, and poor Laura had to go out on the porch, as she faints over every little thing. Injuries, or even talking about them, cause her to turn completely white and faint.

Mom is still stiff and sore, her head is swollen, and she has small cuts all over her forehead. Someone has to help with Dad until her back feels better.

It isn't funny to have an accident. It's so sobering and humiliating. Although we felt thankful, as it could have been so much worse.

Everyone tried to be sympathetic about my legs, but ended up laughing when I said the seat was bent forward in a V where I hit it in the middle, with all that weight. I really hit it hard.

I slept with my mom on Wednesday night, and it really was precious, sitting up talking, and wondering how many years it has been since I slept with her. But, oh my, I slept only a few hours. Mom is the world's "champion snorer." I spent a very miserable night.

She claimed there were bedbugs in her bed, because her legs were itchy in the morning. I told her they were probably evacuating their homes because of threatening thunder above them.

You can't blame the bedbugs. I would have evacuated, too, if I would have known where to go! All in fun, but it was so nice to catch up on sleep over the weekend.

[OCTOBER 14, 1996]

Who Gets the Bed?

Otis is getting bathed a lot lately, and his coat is so shiny; it's blue black.

Andy takes him along up to bed when it's cold outside, and I think it's okay, as I always visualize Andy in his bed and Otis on the sheepskin rug beside him.

Well, it turns out Otis is in bed, and so is Andy. He came down one morning saying he didn't sleep well. Otis had almost the whole bed and he had only a small part.

[OCTOBER 14, 1996]

Beautiful Autumn Days

Leaves fell from the trees in swirling masses after the rain and high winds of yesterday. Trees were at their peak this week, and it was almost hard to see all the pretty leaves fall.

The school spent an afternoon at

Letterkenny Dam on Tuesday. It was one of those bright blue October days, and the scenery was enough to make us all "ohh" and "ahh." When we drove in the lane, the brilliant foliage hung close above the tumbling creek, with the bright blue sky above it. The upper graders promptly took off, climbing to the top of the steep ridge at the side of the dam. So the lower graders and I went for a long walk, gathering leaves and moss, etc.

I almost had the pupils persuaded to just stay at school and have extra recess, because they have so much fun playing in the woods. There is a strip of woods adjacent to the playground, and they sure have spent many hours playing down there. They built houses with logs, and have their little families. We always had a good time playing like that, and as long as there is no mischief, I will let them play there. Although I am aware of the fact that some teachers would frown on me not being on the playground. It is the only time I have to check books, as I have a family at home to spend time with in the evening.

[OCTOBER 20, 1996]

Wedding Time

Well, I just had a very pleasant interruption when Grandma Lydia Byler came and said they are at Emanuels for dinner. So we visited them in the afternoon. Stephen (Debbie) was there too. Grandpas offered to substitute over the weddings if I needed someone. How generous! Of course I must speak with Joe Blank sei MaryAnn, as she offered it too. People are so kindhearted, it just puts me in mind of the little verse, "The world is so full of a number of things, I'm sure we should all be as happy as kings." I'm sure I don't deserve such kindness.

I would suppose there are some very busy people throughout the valley who are preparing for that special day for their daughters. I am looking forward to the weddings, as there I can do two of my favorite things, eat and talk—meeting old friends, and making new ones, and just being happy for the young couple. Marriage is such a precious union, even if we are not prepared for the trials we will face in life. We would want it no other way than to grow old together, and the bond becomes stronger as the years go by.

I am so tickled. I just heard last evening that we are to help some of the younger couples make potatoes at David Blank's wedding. They need someone who is experienced to help along, as they are having one of their huge weddings again. The joy of David's life, and the despair of the married children! No, all in fun, I do believe the children do it gladly, and there is always plenty of food, and it's a well-managed affair even if there are a lot of people. But it really tickles me that we are supposed to supervise the potatoes, because Gid got this really broad grin, which means he will go to the wedding. Hooray, David Blank, you know exactly how to handle him.

[OCTOBER 20, 1996]

Future Baker

Yesterday I stopped at David Flauds to pick up Laura, and Sarah had baked three pans of "creme de menthe" bars and a pan of apple crisp. It looked so perfect and delicious, and Sarah looked so motherly with all her pastries, that I felt totally untalented. Last evening Mom had cream-filled coffee cake, apple cobbler, and a chocolate sheet cake, and they were like pictures. I told Laura when I'm not teaching anymore, I am determined to practice baking until I can. One thing on my list is pumpkin pie. I have never baked one in my life.

[OCTOBER 20, 1996]

Worried Mother

Weddings are still going strong. On Tuesday is Elmer Fisher's, and Laura went to Christ Eshes to their daughter Anna and Amos King's Ike's wedding on Thursday. You can just count me right in with other paranoid mothers who lie awake and worry when their children don't come home. Laura went with Dad Bylers in the morning, and they returned safely at 10:00 without her that evening. Gid had gone hunting, so I couldn't wake him and worry. I lay there telling myself this is ridiculous. Of course she will be home soon and she is perfectly all right. And this is silly; I won't worry. I will not. Aaahh, a car coming. She's coming now. Oh good. How despairing when the car went past. So I got up and paced the floor and watched out the window and thought of all the things that could have happened. Suppose someone forgot her? Suppose she missed the driver? Suppose she has the blues? Too late now for a driver. How (panic) is she gonna come home? Oh, another buggy coming. Here she comes. No, it went right past. Oh, groan. Something has to be wrong. I was too shook up to pray sensibly, so I just sat there in a world of fear and faithlessness, when lo, another buggy. YES! My joy knew no bounds. When she walked in the door, she was so relaxed and happy, totally unruffled. I greeted her with a weak-kneed little squeak, "Laura, where WERE you?" "Mom, what is wrong with you? I just wasn't ready to come home when *Doddys* came, so I came with Reuben." Elmer Fisher's Reuben, bless his heart. I probably would have hugged him for bringing her safely home if I could have. Oh dear, it seems I have a lot to learn yet, and I will get laughed at for this, but I don't care. I want to know where my children are, at least till I get used to it.

[NOVEMBER 10, 1996]

"Who Can Find a Virtuous Woman?"

Well, I feel exactly like a virtuous woman, who rises early and gets a lot accomplished. Sure is different being a virtuous woman. No, seriously, Laura went to help Elmers today and with the usual mountain of Monday laundry, I got up at 4:15 and washed. I normally hate to wash in the dark, but I thought it was fun. Cold and windy, with snow flying, and out of the dark on the other side of the road came this squeaky hollering, "Linda, it's cold and snowing!" There was Mom Byler hanging out her wash too. I taught school like usual, cleaned the schoolhouse and washed the cups from school here at home, got all the wash in and folded it, now I want to make a turkey potpie for supper.

Gid shot a wild turkey on Saturday and quite the best one I have ever eaten. It was almost like the store-bought ones, all tender and juicy.

[NOVEMBER 10, 1996]

Whose Rights?

Andy rode his horse back to the neighboring fields and spotted a 6-point buck and two does. He was so excited to tell Gid that he was actually stuttering. I fail to catch the excitement when it comes to deer hunting. Let the poor things live. But Gid thinks they were made for this purpose. Oops. I better not stick my foot in my mouth again and let some animal rights person read this. Oh, it's indeed a small world, as the *Botschaft* goes far and wide. We have to be careful. No news.

[NOVEMBER 10, 1996]

Rest and Relaxation

After a hectic week, we are enjoying a day at home, which is relaxing. Dad Kauffmans and Jr. and Betty were our supper guests last evening. I had school till lunchtime, in order to make up for one of the three days we had off for weddings. So after cleaning the school, we prepared lasagna, leftover turkey and gravy, mashed potatoes, salad, corn, and date pudding. Laura made brownies, and we made Rice Krispie treats after discovering marshmallows at Petersheims for 30 cents a package. It was a real cozy afternoon in the rain, and the supper turned out well.

[DECEMBER 1, 1996]

Modern-Day Cinderella

Dad is doing well again, with only occasional bouts of feeling weak and tired. Mom, Eva, Ruthie, and Betty are going shopping on Tuesday and will take him along for the day. He really enjoys that, and I'm glad he can go. I won't mention very much how I pity myself, at home teaching school, feeling very much like Cinderella. They all went to Juniata last week to visit with Maryann Weaver at Uncle Tobes, and then I thought about what an excellent martyr I'm getting to be. Now this week I'm bordering on being pitifully deprived. Not seriously, just calling attention to myself.

[DECEMBER 1, 1996]

U.S. Travel

School is certainly not boring this time of year, and it keeps me hopping to get the program ready. We worked at some Christmas art yesterday, and have practiced a few times now. We have quite a few lively ones, and I do believe this will be a good year to have a program.

Everyone was in need of a challenge, so instead of ordinary geography, we are traveling around the U.S., and some of them are going to such faraway places as France and Laos. Their assignment every week is to keep a journal of their surroundings and write a postcard to me. So far, it's been very interesting, and they actually did write realistic stories.

[DECEMBER 1, 1996]

The "Huge Black Dog"

Otis is still out at school every day. This week our neighbor men rode their four-wheelers past, and a collie dog always follows them, running as fast as he can go. For some reason this always upsets poor Otis, and the hair on the back of his neck will rise, and he growls and cries. So we let him in the schoolroom. We were practicing for the program, singing as loudly as we could, and Otis ran and sat beside Rosanne, exactly in line, and smiled as nice as I ever saw him smile, just as well mannered as any child. We kept him in the schoolhouse until the four-wheelers had gone back. Then he was reluctantly let out again. I'm always grateful to the pupils that they accept him so well, as it seems to me at the first grade level, a huge black dog would have scared me.

[DECEMBER 1, 1996]

Teaching Respect to an Equine

Andy has finished training the little pony, and now has an 18-month-old Tennessee Walker. He has ridden her already, but seems to have his problems, as she has no respect whatever for a human being. Andy says she'd walk right over him if he'd try to lead her to the water trough. He loves his horses, and was riding Rusty, his saddle horse, going flat out, across the fields, this afternoon, through a huge puddle, and water sprayed all over the place. Of course, right beside him, tongue hanging out, and bound and determined to keep up, was old Otis. Eli Dad said if we had a bunch of boys, his horses probably wouldn't do as well, but this way they have only one master. Gid just shakes his head and says he sure didn't get it from him.

Not much news this time, which is always the case for me. It is really stormy outside, getting more and more windy. Glad I don't have to go sit in the woods tomorrow morning waiting on some hapless deer.

[DECEMBER 1, 1996]

Christmastime

Christmas is only a pleasant memory now, like colorful candies sprinkled on a cookie, all jumbled with bright instances and circumstances. The program; meeting a van load of Dayton, Virginia, friends; children singing and opening their packages; and Leroy Bert, the driver, handing out candy canes. Cleaning up after the program; having our gifts at home; Andy's face upon opening the long-hoped-for saddle; the girls all curled up reading, reading, reading. Books are always a major Christmas item at our house.

Christmas dinner was at Mom Byler's house, with all the Byler children and grandchildren present, *Doddy* Sam Z.'s included.

Now today we were all at Amos Blanks for the Kauffman side, and we have two sick little girls. Anna and Emily have sore throats and a fever.

Such a whirlwind of activities, and I thoroughly enjoyed every minute. It's such a joyous time, to think of the Christ child being born, all because God loves us and sent a Savior. It's so beautiful and so simple. And this joy is pictured in the faces of the children everywhere on Christmas Day.

[DECEMBER 29, 1996]

Good Ol' Pity Party

Rachel Esh spent Christmas afternoon here with us, and I thought surely between Rachel and me, we could bind and gag Gid and drag him to the singing. Well, I asked twice and Rachel asked very nicely, but he wouldn't budge. So…Dad Bylers came over with Andy's present, a game called "Woods and Water," and as it all turned out Eli Dad, Gid, Andy, and Rachel became very involved in this super game, and I read awhile, then bid everyone good night, and went to bed. I was planning on pitying myself, but I went to sleep too soon.

[DECEMBER 29, 1996]

Teaching

So tomorrow we go back to school, back to ordinary lessons and everyday work. Which I feel sure will be more relaxing than preparing for the program. The children really did a wonderful job, and I have a little reward for them tomorrow.

School is halfway over, and Laura is looking forward to the year after I am finished. And I am ready to become a full-time mother again, I really am.

Last year I would never have been ready to give it up, but for some reason I can easily hand it over to Laura.

I plan on working on my Christmas play book after the holidays. I want to include art, plays, poems, etc., and just see what I can come up with.

[DECEMBER 29, 1996]

Mollie and Becky Again

Mollie Van Lieu is spending a week of her Christmas vacation here again. Becky is always so excited when her dad brings her. They're planning on sleeping in Laura's bed, and "surprising" her when she gets home tonight after the singing. They might be dumped unceremoniously out of their warm quarters, which is what they're probably hoping will happen.

Those two girls think of everything, and they are always finding something exciting to do.

[DECEMBER 29, 1996]

End of Baseball Career

Myriads of Concoctions

Israel Stotzfuses spent New Year's in Wayne County, Indiana, with Ivan and Sara, visiting relatives. We have little Stephen, and he was so excited to spend the day at our house. Unfortunately, he woke up feeling miserable, with a headache and fever. Poor little guy turned out to be really sick, with high fever and being delirious that night.

This flu sure has made lots of people miserable, big ones and little ones alike. All these remedies and advice on what to do kind of leaves your head swimming. Is it cold water on the forehead, and feet in warm water? I guess, 'cause sticking your head in warm water could drown a person eventually. Honey and lemon for the throat, and vinegar in a hot bath. Or is the honey for the bathtub and the vinegar mixed with lemon?

Lemon and vinegar would soon serve a purpose one way or another, either put you out of your misery or you'd feel better after you drank it, simply because you quit drinking it. I hardly believe in anything, and when I'm sick, I am just an unbearable old grouch till the virus leaves. I try and tend to the children, though, but I'm not a motherly person who hovers over them with all kinds of concoctions.

[JANUARY 6, 1997]

"Not-Too-Bad" Pies

On Thursday Laura taught while I spent the day at home, cooking and baking up a storm, as we had supper for the steelworkers.

I debated whether I just wanted to ask Leah to make cherry pies, but, no (I had this surge of self-confidence again), I can do it.

Measuring, mixing, stirring, patching torn holes in the pie crust, but the result was three "not-too-bad" pies ready for the oven. So I whip them into the oven, whistling a catchy tune, and twirling around the kitchen, feeling perfectly in charge.

Homemade baked beans, fry the bacon, tweedle-dee, the happy chef enjoying a day in the kitchen. Oh no, a definite funny smell.

The pies. Arrrgghh! The juice is running all over the place, and the pies are too brown.

So I yanked them out and plopped them on the counter, the ugly old things. That evening I couldn't help noticing that only one measly piece of cherry pie was eaten. David Byler ate it. I remember now. Thank you, David, you'll never know what you did to my thoroughly smashed ego!

[JANUARY 6, 1997]

Delectable Cat Food

Mollie and Becky had a wonderful week together again. On Thursday Becky decided they weren't going to eat till supper, and they didn't. They cut cheese, helped clean vegetables, and did not taste anything.

After a while I heard Mollie ask Becky if she was out in the barn. Becky said, "No," and Mollie followed up with, "Yes, you were, Becky. You were out there eating cat food." She was dead serious, in the most accusing tone of voice. I laughed till I almost had to cry. It was so funny how hungry and grouchy they actually were.

[JANUARY 6, 1997]

Aches, Pains, Bruises, and More

Brrr! Zero degrees and everyone dashes to the mailbox, dashes around to do chores, and scuttles down the road to school, all except the hardy souls who venture out to go skating.

Joe Blank's Rebecca and Gideon came to go skating with the girls and Rebecca fell on the ice, receiving a serious gash close to her eye, requiring five stitches. What excitement! Andy scootered her home, while poor Gideon was left to fend for himself. He took off as the crow flies, straight across the fields, and related his journey with a huge smile the next morning.

. . . . .

That same evening Laura went to get her new contact lenses. Coming home, the pain was severe, and we tried in vain to find the cause of her intense pain. No use. We had to take her right back to the doctor, and he discovered she had a very irritated cornea from wearing her contacts too long. Oh dear, what an evening!

. . . . .

The following day Israel's James fell while ice skating at school and was a very sick boy that evening with a severe headache and nausea. He was absent the next day, resting at Grandma Kauffmans (where Eva had gone to stay with Dad), while Mom, Ruthie, and I went to Petersheim's store.

. . . . .

That same morning, Rosanne was crying, having a fever and a sore side. But because of all the skating, I dismissed the side as "she probably fell on the ice." It was hard to go to school that morning, but I left her in Laura's care, only to find one miserable little person that evening. Her fever had escalated, and she cried as soon as she saw me because of the pain. I simply cried with her—poor, neglected little soul. I could only think of appendicitis and hurried to get her to the doctor's office before 4:00, as the lab technician went home then. Evidently they decide a lot by taking blood if it's appendicitis or not. We had Dr. Bill Freeman, who is always very thorough, and he thought the pain was too far toward her back to be her appendix, and had a urine sample done. She had a kidney infection, and he made it sound very serious. If she would not have improved by morning she would have had to be put on IV, as kidneys can be serious. Poor girl, then she fainted in the lab while having her blood work done, and the whole evening was quite an ordeal for her. She was kept quiet for 24 hours, and the medicine did the trick.

. . . . .

Dan Stoltzfus's Miriam, who is nine years old, had her tonsils and adenoids removed last week. Rosanne had the utmost sympathy for her, but we heard Miriam really fared better than some children do. I'm sure they, too, are relieved that the operation is over.

[JANUARY 20, 1997]

Who's Eating the Letters

I guess I'll just have to make a huge, unhappy fuss about the post office, mail carrier, *Botschaft* office, all the workers, and life in general. Where are my last two letters? I am mentally hopping up and down, face red and hollering out my indignation. I never do anything wrong myself, so why should these people? Seriously, I would never berate anyone about the loss of a few letters, but I do wonder who skipped breakfast and ate my letters instead.

[JANUARY 20, 1997]

Snitching a Few Bites

Elmer Fishers, Matthews, and Levi Kings were our supper guests last evening. I put a small turkey in the oven in the morning, and Andy and Daniel Flaud's David Alan beat us home. I found two pot holders and two forks beside the oven, and I thought surely I would open the roaster to find a pile of bones! They just helped themselves very nicely to a huge breast portion and went skating at Levi Eshes. The fourteen- and fifteen-year-olds had a hockey game there, and it sounded absolutely thrilling. But

David Alan did receive a huge gash in his lip, and I'm wondering if he didn't need stitches, too. Levi's Lena brought cookies, brownies, and warm, freshly made soft pretzels down to the pond. Andy claimed he never in all his life ate anything so good. They must have been delicious, as Andy's description of the boys grabbing them reminded me of a school of piranhas in a tropical river.

We're supposed to have a surprise visit by the school board today, but I kind of guessed that's who is coming. So I must go sweep and make everything appear perfect for them. I can't have them thinking I'm not a good teacher.

[JANUARY 20, 1997]

Winter Activities

Mommy, Eva Kauffman, and B.B. sei Eva stopped in for a brief chat on Friday. Eva had been staying with Grandma awhile, because Ben Lantzes are in Mexico. Eva pointed out what a good location we have for a school, with a hill to go sledding, a pond, and a woods. And it's true, we do have it so nice. The pond is an enormous distraction to all school work. The boys play hockey, and the girls started to set lunches in a row, jumping them, until they were up to ten lunches! They are all good skaters, and thoroughly enjoy their sport.

So the winter days are going by, and before we know it, spring will be here. I am looking forward to digging in—housecleaning, yard work, etc.—and getting some real good exercise.

[JANUARY 26, 1997]

Home Alone

Gid is on stay-away again. They are building a garbage recycling plant in Virginia, and he enjoys his work. We have it made when he's on stay-away. Doesn't that sound awful? I mean, we eat crazy stuff for supper, whenever we want, and sleep till 7:00 in the morning. I used to feel guilty about not minding when he goes for a week, but everyone is different. I am not as dependent as some women, and can be happily independent for weeks at a time. We miss each other by Friday evening though, but we have fun during the week. We make cream of wheat or tacos or cereal or sometimes just bagels for supper. And when Gid is here, I always make a big supper, 'cause he carries his lunch.

[JANUARY 26, 1997]

Poor Rosanne

Rosanne fell on Friday morning coming to school and landed on her face. She had brush burns and a huge swollen mouth, and seemingly could not be comforted, so I sent her home to lie on the couch. There was a whole group of sympathetic little friends standing with me, and I commented, "Poor Rosanne. She's so skinny and kind of homely and has all the tough luck, it seems."

Her cousin, Israel's Stephen, wisely rolled his

eyes and firmly declared, "She is NOT homely." It was so cute, because Eva told me when Stephen discovered that you cannot marry your first cousin, he was deeply disappointed. He had confided to his mother that someday he would marry Rosanne. She's such an easygoing little individual, and never showed much self-will since the day she was born, and gets along with everyone. Stephen and Rosanne are in first and second grade!

[JANUARY 26, 1997]

Amish "Betty Crocker"

I had Eva's name for Christmas, and gave her a cookbook. She loves to bake, and always has.

Last night she sent over a sample of lemon sponge, shoofly, and apple crumb pie, all from this cookbook. It is unbelievable that I am even remotely related to this Amish "Betty Crocker." You should taste them!

I am really watching my diet again, and it was the despair of me. Oh well, Eva, all the while I was inhaling the lemon sponge pie (my favorite) I kept assuring myself that I could skate better than you, and had better scores in school. Wasn't it something else yet? All in fun, but the pies were absolutely wonderful.

[JANUARY 26, 1997]

The Supper Gang

Sunday morning Laura asked me if there would be a possibility that we could make supper for the youth, as there was nothing planned. Of course, I thought so, but there's always the "big hurdle." Gid! Well, Laura asked nicely and the argument started, with Andy chipping in on Gid's side. Of course, I stuck up for Laura, and our winning argument was that they really don't mind having the youth as much as they are embarrassed by their sloppy shop and barn.

By the time we left for church, we reached a peaceful compromise. If no one else had anything planned, we would provide supper. And so we did.

Kind helpers sure were needed, as I never had a supper gang. Ben Kurtzes, Israels, David Flauds, and John Beilers all came, too. Fannie brought an angel food cake and paper plates and cups. Eva brought pudding. I had a cake on hand, and we mixed peaches, pears, and bananas. Laura and Ruthie stopped at the freezer and got hamburger and creamed corn, and our menu was barbecue sandwiches, creamed potatoes, corn, macaronis, and a salad, with a head of lettuce borrowed from Rhoda. We had way too much of everything, but after filling Cool Whip containers for everyone that helped, I can freeze the barbecue. We really enjoyed having them, and I commented to Gid how much we have to be thankful for. We don't want to lose these supper gangs, as to Gid and me, who were never used to being with the parents at supper, it is really something.

I know there is plenty to be concerned about, and we are, but we have much to be grateful for.

[FEBRUARY 3, 1997]

Brown Fuzzy Wall

After listening to Becky's complaints about the wallpaper in her bedroom for two years, I now decided we'll see if we can pull it off. Becky is a little person with a huge mind, an overactive imagination, and just wilts and gets miserable and unhappy without a goal, or something that holds her interest. She needs something to keep her occupied, and it has to be a challenge. So I tentatively pulled on one corner of the wallpaper, only to shake my head and tell her she may as well give up. "Well, it's off, Mom," was her quick reply, "but what's that brown fuzzy stuff?" The brown fuzzy stuff was no less than half the paper. In defeat I told her just to move her room.

She wanted me to call a wallpaper place, which I did, and he said our only alternative is to wet it, let it soak, and peel it off. That was all Becky needed. Armed with a Windex bottle, she set to work. The top part stripped right off, but, oh, the monumental task of removing the brown fuzzy stuff. Laura helped her, and I did a tiny bit, but it just depressed me, how slowly the whole room got done. She worked for almost a week, until Saturday, using sandpaper to make it smooth. We applied a coat of primer and the leftover off-white paint from Laura's room. What a pleased Becky! With hard work and lots of effort, she has the desired results. Gid was not too happy about our project, until he went up to check on her progress. He came down, laughing and shaking his head. She was sitting in the middle of a pile of wet crumbly paper, patiently doing one spot at a time.

[FEBRUARY 3, 1997]

Fisher's Menagerie

Becky and Andy were at Joe Blanks on Saturday evening to play "Woods and Water." The boys slept in the haymow and thought it was so fun. Becky and Becca went over to Alvin Fishers, where they found their three-year-old Eva Lynn rocking a baby rabbit dressed in doll clothes, sound asleep, with a doll bag at her side. On her shoulder perched a blue parakeet, and Becky had a fit about this house full of animals. She promptly purchased two rabbits of her own. Alvins also have a deaf Dalmatian puppy she fell in love with.

[FEBRUARY 11, 1997]

Breakfast Hosts

On Sunday we were privileged to have a group of young people who were there for the night. I made piles of pancakes, two dozen eggs, ham, and a stack of toast, besides a gallon of orange juice. We're totally new at this, just "fledgling" parents of teenagers, but we thoroughly enjoyed having them. I appreciated their friendliness, and it was so nice to have them with us. They all left for the supper gang and singing, which was a good fifteen-mile trek. Now that would be me a "trouble," as we say in Dutch, but I remember the times when a long buggy ride was really a thrill.

[FEBRUARY 11, 1997]

How Embarrassing!

On Thursday, Mom and Ruthie asked if I wanted to go along to Wal-Mart and Hillside Fabrics. Laura is always willing to teach, but I still felt guilty, like I was playing hooky or whatever. But I couldn't give it up, so I took Emily along. She complained of stomachache while I combed her hair, but I thought she'll be okay. Peacefully walking along the Wal-Mart aisles with Emily, she threw up without warning. Oh dear, what an embarrassing situation.

Red-faced and totally humiliated, I mopped wildly with a few Kleenexes, and in desperation, her sweater. I scuttled to the restroom, feeling, oh, so low classed, and proceeded to wash her dress with soap and water. I tried to dry it under the hand dryer, with no luck, so I bought a little sweatshirt and pants for her. At the checkout, the lady took pity on this poor shivering child, and changed her in the restroom while I paid my bill. Poor Emily. I wondered how many people were mad at this fat, red-faced Amish lady with her shivering, pale, undernourished child? So after a few explanations to Mom and Ruthie, I hurried out to the van with my little "English" daughter, to find John Esh parked behind the van! He was smiling and waving, but I felt I must explain to him that I still believe in dressing my children Amish!

It turned out to be a nerve-wracking trip, and I was ever so glad to return home. Sometimes when you have a feeling you shouldn't go, you better listen to the good little guy perched on your shoulder!

. . . . . .

I must run along. There are many different things to be done today. We want to have a mystery dinner at school on Friday for Valentine's Day. Maybe Gid will bring me a dozen roses home from Virginia!

[FEBRUARY 11, 1997]

Steelworker Fatality

We were surprised to have Gid return from Virginia on Thursday evening, but soon learned why he was home a day early. A welder from another construction crew was welding a huge counterweight that had been filled with concrete the previous day. The sparks ignited somewhere, and our men were all subject to watch this man being hurled into the air, turning three somersaults, hitting a twenty-foot wall, and coming to rest on the ground not far from them. It was a very subdued bunch who had to answer questions for the authorities, and the job site was shut down till Monday. It must have been quite an experience for them to witness this, although Gid said he was killed instantly, because of the explosion ripping through his face. Definitely, this steelwork is far more dangerous than the agricultural construction, as this is the third person in about a year. Safety harnesses are necessary, even if sometimes cumbersome.

[FEBRUARY 18, 1997]

Becky's Bunny Cottage

Becky bought rabbits from Alvin Fisher's Marianne. Now, this is no ordinary "put a few rabbits in a cage and feed them" kind of thing. First, Dad brought the playhouse up from the barn, where Andy had his pigeons. Then she planned to have a flower bed and vegetable garden around the playhouse, where her rabbits will be reclining in greatest luxury. This project definitely needed a phone call to Mollie in East Berlin. Mollie will contribute a welcome mat and a wreath for the door, curtains, shavings, and marigold seeds. The playhouse is now being named a cottage. Somehow I seem to think of those rabbits lolling on a lounging chair, with sunglasses and a glass of iced tea and a fan to cool themselves comfortably! Becky spends every spare hour feverishly cleaning this filthy old pigeon house. As long as she is happy and occupied, so are we.

[FEBRUARY 18, 1997]

The Ugly Dress

Last night, Becky was really on a roll. Talking a mile a minute, totally enthused, reading things to Laura. It was Monday night and Laura is not very enthused or friendly Monday evenings. I was cutting a dress for her, and as usual, Becky's eyes narrowed and she commented, "I hate that color. What a stupid dress. What fails you, Laura?" I could see that Laura's patience was wearing thin, but she said that Grandmother gave it to her. Becky kept fussing till Laura shut her up with, "Well, GOOD, Becky. I'm glad that I have an ugly dress." What could she say? She wandered off to read, and we resumed cutting in peace.

[FEBRUARY 18, 1997]

Winding Down

We had a mystery dinner at school on Valentine's Day. We exchanged valentines and played games and had story time in the afternoon. Our next goal and something to look forward to, after they have 750 hundred percents, is to go to Lancaster, visiting schools.

. . . . .

As the school year winds down, I feel a bit reluctant to quit again. But Laura is planning on starting at Elmer's greenhouse March 1st, so after those few hectic months are over I'll probably be quite ready to quit.

[FEBRUARY 18, 1997]

Migraine Victim

Andy is at home with another migraine headache. He has been a very miserable person lately, having one migraine after another, throwing up almost every day. He was thrown from one of his horses, hitting the manger with his ribs, so I'm wondering if perhaps a good chiropractor could help him. Pain relievers don't do a thing for a full-blown migraine. We've been advised to closely watch his diet, and does he need glasses? So if these attacks persist, my first choice would be my friendly chiropractor, Dr. Burkholder, in town.

[MARCH 3, 1997]

It's Cold!

We stayed at Amoses for supper last evening, and feeling the need for some exercise after Ruthie's delicious lasagna, Becky, Joe's Becca, and I walked home. I warned the girls about being cold; they'll need their shawls and bonnets. They didn't think so. Well, we must have been a funny sight, walking uphill and down, through woods, a small town, over a bridge, with a lady wearing a bonnet, in her Sunday best, and two girls sharing the shawl! They were freezing, and since my body was well fueled by overeating, the bonnet was sufficient. Finally the girls decided it would be better to take turns with the shawl, and a certain telephone pole or sidewalk was the place to switch from comfort to goose pimples!

[MARCH 3, 1997]

Laura

Laura is supposed to start at Elmer's greenhouse today, but since we are having a spring blizzard, she will likely go tomorrow. Her hours are from 1:00 in the afternoon till dark. She takes her supper and scooters every day, watching the greenhouse so Elmers can have supper together. She is really looking forward to it, and it will do her good to get out and have more to do after washing, watching Kendall and Emily, and reading books. She is an avid reader and always seems to have her nose in a book. I always hoped she'd take an interest in sewing, but woe is me, she's exactly like her mother in that respect, sewing only what is necessary and being very glad when it's done.

[MARCH 3, 1997]

The Need to Socialize

What a beautiful morning! Several inches of snow fell during the night, and the warm sun and a chilly wind are both trying to master the snow. Well, sorry, chilly winds, but it is soon the middle of March.

Yesterday we were invited to Emanuel and Barbara's for breakfast, to Ike Kings for dinner (but they went to Dauphin County, so I suppose she wasn't serious), and Israels invited all the families who usually attend buddies' day. Gid was talking about going to Aaron Eshes, but that's as far as he got. Too many people at Israels he claimed, although Andy and I gave him a healthy argument. He says he doesn't have any buddies, so why would he go? Once a hermit, always a hermit. I said, and I mean this, everyone on this earth has a need to socialize with other people. He has his crews to talk to all week, and all the men he works with. No wonder it doesn't bother him.

[MARCH 10, 1997]

Good, Submissive Wife

So, all right, all the children started to clamor about going to the Shippensburg Reservoir back at Roxbury.

We packed a picnic lunch, and one skinny little sleeping bag, and wearing only coats and sweaters against the surprisingly brisk breeze, we set off. To make a long story short, the children had so much fun. It is really beautiful back there, and it was a lovely family outing.

Now shall I say the real part?

I was so cold, and Emily was shivering, and inside I still wanted to be at Israels. But I was determined to now, for once, be totally submissive for real. And I was. I did a wonderful job on the submitting, and lay on the sleeping bag reading a book and eating barbecue chips, until the sun subtly hid behind gray clouds, and the goose pimples started up my spine. The children were collecting moss, chasing each other, and they didn't think about it. Brrrr! Gid looked as content as a cow chewing her cud, and all of a sudden I got up and stamped around, barking how I wish we'd be like ordinary people and be at Israels and it's too COLD to go on a picnic. Gid just stared at me and kind of chuckled, till I had to laugh, too.

The girls collected moss, and two pieces look like turtles. They're named Timmy and Tammy Turtle, and are all snuggled in a cheese box. The wedding will be tonight, and when they die, they will build coffins and bury them. In all sincerity, I hope Timmy and Tammy enjoy a long and happy married life.

[MARCH 10, 1997]

At the Raise of a Paw

A feisty little beagle visited school and had Otis in quite an uproar, so Andy brought him inside. It was Friday afternoon, everyone was having art, and Otis was sitting in a seat right behind Andy. He just sat there, looking intently at me. It looked so human, it made me feel crazy. Almost as if Otis was going to raise his hand, I mean, paw, and ask for a picture and some crayons. Everyone is so used to Otis, they turned around and laughed a bit, but resumed their coloring, thinking it's just Otis, and it's hard telling what he'll do.

[MARCH 10, 1997]

How Wide?

Dad Bylers visited Alphaus Speichers yesterday, after hearing the injury he received on his hand. They also visited *Doddy* Sam Bylers and stopped at Stephen Lees. They came over to tell us about the "adventures." We sat all cuddled up, trying to thaw out after our frigid picnic, and they looked so young and happy. I told Gid they really enjoy going to visit people, and it makes them feel good. Gid heartily agreed with me. Now wasn't that nice? Maybe by the time we're 60 years old, we'll be happily trotting all over Franklin County, visiting people.

Perhaps not, as Gid keeps telling people that I'm getting so wide, he's going to have to sit out on the mirror when we're older. There's no room for him in the front seat.

Wouldn't that be a sight?

[MARCH 10, 1997]

Mixed-Up Morning

On Thursday Mom Kauffman, Israel sei Eva, and I took nine upper graders to Lancaster to visit schools. We had a really wonderful day, after our "crazy" beginning. Miriam Smith was scheduled to pick us up at 6:00. The driver was a little early. It was Mike Jr., and Mom was along. Oh well, change of plans, no big deal, so we went to pick up Eva. After she was picked up, Mike mentioned something about Amos King telling him what time. Amos King! So we figured out he picked up the wrong person and he was getting the wrong load. We had a hectic half hour trying to locate Miriam. Mike Jr. stopped at Amos Blanks instead of neighbor Aquillas to get Florence. All Blanks to him!

We visited Mary Fisher's school, Verna Fisher's, the Gordonville Bookstore, Lizzie Fisher's, and Emma Hoover's. What an inspiring day! It was especially interesting for Laura, who has never seen other teachers' methods, as Marianne Zimmerman was her teacher all eight years.

We had been trying to reach a goal of 750 100%s for a few months, and that was the reward. Gideon Blank and Suzanne Fisher, who are in the third grade, also helped, but decided to stay home, so they received a nice prize, and everything worked out alright.

[MARCH 17, 1997]

The Rabbit People

Becky's rabbits have a habit of opening their own door and hopping to freedom. She is quite frustrated, but somehow it only seems natural for these little rabbit "people" to open their own doors. She has the wildest ideas for the most beautiful flower and vegetable gardens around the rabbit "duplex." Guess who will probably keep it looking nice?

[MARCH 17, 1997]

Horse Trainer Andy

Andy didn't go along to Lancaster to visit schools. He almost panicked at the thought, so knowing the day would probably go more smoothly minus Andy, we left him at home. He's getting bored with no horses to train. He had made a nice amount of money training them for Ronnie Weaver.

He was fussing to me this morning about getting Dad Byler's beautiful colt to train. "To drive?" I snorted. "You never trained a horse to drive." He promptly told me he'll never know unless he tries. Dad Byler must have a lot of trust in Andy's ability. So now Andy's head is somewhere in the region of the clouds, daydreaming of having his own horse and buggy. In about a year, he'll be needing one, so between daydreaming and building peacock pens in his mind, equations and vocabulary come in way last. SIGH.

[MARCH 17, 1997]

Early Birds

Already it is Tuesday. I always write this letter on Monday, but I suppose the day was too full, or else I just didn't manage right. I guess teaching school, folding loads of clothes, washing, lunches, planting garden, raking, and getting supper before I plopped wearily on the recliner with a good book deserves to be called a day.

I can hardly believe my good fortune this year, in having the opportunity to be classed with the early birds. I sure am feeling smart. Two pounds of peas and radishes and onions planted, and it's the last week in March. Usually we don't have such good management, so we will see if I get a bumper crop of peas. Becky planted her garden around the rabbit cottage, and we planned the flower beds. Her rabbits are so adorable, and she shoveled fresh sand into the "screened patio"! It was such a pure pleasure to work outside, and I loved every minute of it.

[MARCH 25, 1997]

Avid Reader

The Franklin County bookmobile stops at the Lurgan Greenhouse, so Laura came home from work with a scooter basket filled with books. They are usually about the lives of teenagers, but I find them so interesting.

She picks out the Newberry Award Winners, and they are usually so well written. So with Gid in Virginia again, I sit and read in the evening. The *National Geographic* and the *U.S. News* don't last long enough, and I very seldom find a book that holds my interest too long.

Some books are so artificial or whatever, and to me, it seems like a play, and it's hard to stay interested. But every once in a while I will find a "real" book that holds my undivided attention for an entire evening.

[MARCH 25, 1997]

School Pet

Emily is being juggled back and forth from home to school, usually at lunchtime. She's a happy little individual who loves to come to school as long as she has a snack whenever she gets hungry. She'll sit all by herself in a huge desk, chomping on potato chips while I have classes.

Needless to say, she's the school's pet, and everyone wants her to sit with them. In singing class, she'll be firmly wedged between Anna and Becky, belting out her version of all the songs.

Ruthie is keeping Kendall for us till school is over. Laura misses her so much, so the other Friday they brought her in the forenoon. They had quite a happy reunion, between Laura, Emily, and Kendall.

[MARCH 25, 1997]

Last Day!!!!!!!

Molly Van Lieu is coming to stay over the Easter holidays again. They have every minute jammed full of plans again. Help Grandma Kauffman make Easter eggs, fix up and paint the rabbit cottage, go to the Shippensburg Reservoir, and on and on. They better include "helping Mom," because Laura works on Saturdays.

. . . . .

When I taught last year at Otterbein, a former teacher had written in a record book, "Last Day!" with a bunch of exclamation marks. I thought it was awful. But guess who will include about fifty exclamation marks in her record book this year!??

[MARCH 25, 1997]

Shot in the Eye

Israel's Joseph (fifth grade) was hit directly in the eye by a blunt-tipped homemade arrow. The boys have been making these at school, and it did bother me, but they were so engrossed in their project, so I warned them, but let them go. Is there any feeling more sickening than remorse? I heard this shriek, and Joe staggered in followed by Andy, who had shot the arrow. I took one look at his dilated pupil and bloody eye and started to sob. I completely "lost it." Eyes are so precious, and I imagined the worst, feeling so horribly guilty for allowing the boys to have the bows at all.

Becky shot off down the road on a scooter to call a driver, and I just sat on the porch, hugging Joseph and crying. We took him home, and Israels took him to the doctor. Israel said he thinks the eye is bruised, but not really penetrated. When I got back to school, I found Andy sobbing at his desk, everyone white-faced and sober. Little Cheryl promptly started a get well card. So now the bows and arrows are in the trash and we must think of another project.

On the way home. Rosanne said she fell to the floor, completely passed out, when it happened. Poor girl! Another Laura, I guess. Now I'm anxious to hear how Joseph will be tomorrow.

[MARCH 25, 1997]

Women's Rights

Did we ever have a mini blizzard on Easter Monday before? What a night! Snow squalls and high winds sure made you forget it was Easter.

Our services were held at Israels on Sunday. God's word was brought by Ben Kurtz and Jacob Fisher. Ben Stoltzfus of east district read the scripture. Dan Stoltzfuses of north district and a few of the youth were our visitors. Nine of our families, including all the Blanks, were missing, so it seemed like a quiet little group. We stayed for supper, and after supper Gid was ready to leave. I wanted to stay for the singing, as we haven't attended any since Laura is with the youth. Well, he wasn't going to stay. So I said, "Fine. I'll stay and go home with Amoses." Gulp. Time for a little women's rights here, I thought self-righteously. It was time to take Dad home, so Amos took Charlie, our horse, and Gid settled in with another cup of coffee and stayed for the singing, too! That was a rare treat, and I was still singing those beautiful songs at the washing machine on Monday morning. I gave Gid a big smile and profusely thanked him for staying. He was assuring Andy that there were just too many people, and he isn't known to prefer that.

[APRIL 2, 1997]

Mollie Comes Again

Gid and Andy were attending to some business, so they picked me up in the afternoon. Phil Van Lieus brought supper that afternoon when they came to pick up Mollie. Mollie spent the Easter holidays with us again, and they worked hard, painting the rabbit cottage a rustic red with dark tan trim. It looks so cute now. Mollie brought an expensive pewter wind chime for the door, a waterer, and a little block of salt. They cleaned and rearranged and fussed and stewed over their little house, but it's too early to start the flower beds.

Laura works at the greenhouse on Saturdays, so Mollie and Becky packed a picnic lunch and walked up to buy a few plants. Elmers were busy, so they kept them to help carry plants for customers. So there I was, all the cleaning, wash to fold, baking, work outside, all by myself. No girls. Well, I was really charged up in the morning. What a challenge to see how much I can do in a day! Well, I whistled and bustled, scrubbed and cleaned and baked. Yuck! I folded clothes, and after lunch I started digging flower beds. What total bliss! Or, as the hours wore on, what total blisters! My soft teacher hands were rudely introduced to the shovel handle, and ouch, when those blisters pop. And, along with popped blisters, I was greatly deflated by 4:00. Completely worn out. I moaned and groaned with stiff shoulders and arms, but it was worth it, with even borders and flower beds ready for flowers.

[APRIL 2, 1997]

Attitude Adjustment

The children are all eagerly looking forward to summer vacation. Only six more weeks of school. After that, life looks like one delight to Andy. He's so grouchy today, and needs a good old-fashioned attitude adjustment after this long weekend.

Joseph's eye is bruised severely, and he needs a doctor's visit almost every day. He is unable to come to school because of drops being administered every hour, but he can see, and hopefully, all will be well. Thank the good Lord!

[APRIL 2, 1997]

End of Baseball Career

My baseball career has come to a screeching halt, and I mean it. On Thursday one of the big boys hit the ball directly into my leg. Ouch, but okay, I'm a big girl. I kept on playing. A few minutes later, another big boy hit it straight into my ankle. Now that was enough. I yelped and limped to the porch and just sat there in agony. Ouch!

The children happily shouted, "Carrom!" and raced for the schoolhouse. I hollered something about why they can't play one thing without me, and they better get out there and play ball. But I do admit defeat. I'm definitely no quick teenager anymore, and this is it. I can't force them to keep playing if they have no interest.

On Friday, Laura taught because she had off work, and there was so much for me to do around the house. So I stayed home; washing, cleaning, and trying to do everything in one day.

And they played and played baseball! Hollering and yelling enthusiastically, competing furiously and thoroughly enjoying their recess. That's where a younger teacher has an advantage, I suppose. That same day I surprised Laura and housecleaned her room. I was pulling on an oak shelf to remove it from the wall, when suddenly the nail tore loose, and crash, into my right eye. I literally saw stars, and sat on the bed feeling like crying, "Waaah." Two huge purple bruises on my leg, limping around so totally overworked, and then that yet!

[APRIL 7, 1997]

Birdhouses, Peacocks, and Fishing

Andy never goes to bed on Friday night before Gid comes home. We sit up together till about 10:30, and when Gid comes, I can never get a word in edgewise. So I wait till every item is thoroughly discussed before I start. This week it was birdhouses (he made a bunch for Ervin Zimmerman's greenhouse), peacocks (they could have a bunch if they could catch them), and fishing.

Saturday afternoon they went fishing and caught a nice bunch of bass and bluegills. Gid's mom is fond of fish, so I invited Dad Bylers and Emanuels for supper. Some of our English friends stopped by, so they joined us too. It was interesting, the men playing croquet, and we ladies just visiting.

[APRIL 7, 1997]

Will You Marry Me?

Becky had her first proposal! Little four-year-old Taran asked her to marry him! Becky accepted gladly, and she is still shaking her head about this little individual. He lives in an adult world. The only child, etc. and is extremely bright.

Becky thoroughly enjoyed him, giving him a ride on Chocolate, showing him the newborn kittens, the rabbit cottage, etc.

His love for Becky must have been monumental, to favor her with a proposal!

. . . . .

I don't have time to sit here writing. I have some checking to do, and windows to wash, and art to remove. Easter is over now, so we need some spring art. The children are working on maps of different states, which makes a nice hall display.

[APRIL 7, 1997]

Don't You Touch Them!

Emily can tie her own shoes, and she's four years old. I asked her who taught her and of course made a fuss. She took a deep breath and told me she wanted to go out, but she was mad at Laura and didn't want Laura near her shoes. So she learned to tie her own, rather than having Laura close! She finished with a very mature roll of her eye, saying, "I don't tie shoes like the rest of the family." I agree, it isn't quite right.

[APRIL 14, 1997]

Floating Horse

It almost brings tears to my eyes to write this, but Eli Dad is letting Andy train the really pretty Cleveland Bay colt. She'll be two years old in May, and is quite a handful. Although Andy loves to spend as much time with her as he can, she still has a stubborn streak. It will be interesting to see how this all turns out. He will be given the chance to buy her, and have her for his own. He gets emotional to talk about her in action. He says she floats instead of trotting, it's so effortless. Her mother is like that, too. Totally blind, and a fast trot with hardly any effort.

[APRIL 14, 1997]

A Visit to Otterbein

Yesterday the whole school walked to Otterbein for a visit—twenty children walking by twos, trying to stay in line, not too fast, not too slow. I kind of felt like Moses, bringing up the rear with Emily.

We enjoyed it, and it was interesting for the children to listen to all the poems and songs. A lot of my children attended Otterbein last year, and the schoolhouse looks entirely different. So much more open and light, with only 22 pupils. I just had to smile to myself, wondering how we got 35 pupils in there with that huge furnace, paper all over the floor, noisy, etc.!

Our books are all being finished, and we still have three more weeks of ordinary work. We have only a few pages in lots of subjects, and everyone is getting bored. I guess we'll make a yearbook to keep at school, with each child's art, stories, and penmanship as a remembrance of the year.

[APRIL 22, 1997]

To Teach or Not to Teach

Last week a load of teachers and pupils visited school, and I must really have been shook up, because I forgot to give them the guest book. That really spited me! But, oh well, I still know they were here and it was so precious. I was asked last week why I don't just continue teaching (by a teacher) and if I would recommend teaching for a mother (by a mother).

I can easily explain by saying, if I was an unmarried person, I would teach. That would be my life, as I love the school environment, the children, etc. But I cannot honestly say I would recommend it for a mother anymore. Even if the work at home gets done in the evening, you are not a mother in the best terms of "mother." As I think back over these two years, I missed out on the things that used to be important to me. Little treats, the time to sit and rock, the silliness and playing with my little ones, just simply those times when you were relaxed.

Our children need to feel loved and cherished, and they need our time. I am a firm believer in a good old-fashioned paddle, have used it often, and can't imagine raising a family without it. But they do have a void in their life, if true love, companionship, trust, and joy, administered by and with their parents, is lacking. And as they grow, they will seek to fill this void with something else. Especially in their teenage years.

[APRIL 22, 1997]

Vanity of Vanities

Emily is probably lacking in something, as the other day while I was housecleaning the bedroom, she stood gazing at herself in the mirror. Turning her head this way and that, she smiled, grimaced, tilted her chin, and rolled her eyes. She said, "I love to look at myself in the mirror. I'm so interesting." She pondered that statement, and tittered, "I bet I shouldn't say that."

[APRIL 22, 1997]

Quite a Contraption

Andy made a boat. He took a plastic 50-gallon drum, cut it in half, cut out the ends, screwed it together, caulked it, put outriggers on it, and made two oars. Quite a contraption. So he took it to our neighbor's pond, and tried it out. The neighbor men stood on the bank, and in Andy's words, "Roared and laughed."

He tried to laugh, but I think he was kind of hurt. He has a trip planned down the Conoduguinet with Israel's boys, and this is the boat he will use.

Becky tried it, too, and dubbed it okay as long as you don't mind a wet "sitter."

[APRIL 22, 1997]

Not Quite Perfect

We had lovely weather this week, so Laura took advantage of it and mulched, planted petunias, and made borders all day. Everyone was tired, so we ate out on the patio, just as the sun was slipping behind the mountain—a perfect setting for a perfect family. Unfortunately we are just not very perfect. No Dad to keep everyone straight, and Laura and Becky in one of their moods.

It all started by picking out peanuts from Rocky Road ice cream, which turned into an all-out knock-down fight for peanuts. I got up and started to pinch girls in earnest. Things were simply getting out of hand, when Andy walked up from the barn with his huge pigeon-catching net. Instantly Laura and I told him to get Becky. She was soon reduced to a curled-up little pile on the patio floor, under the net, with Andy in total control. We did dishes together afterward, and while I missed Gid, I still feel so thankful for this time in our life. A family is so much fun with older children. Hopefully, when school is over, we can relax together more again.

[MAY 5, 1997]

Deeply Embedded Thorn

Andy sees the light at the end of his dark tunnel. School has always been his "thorn in the flesh" and that thorn was imbedded pretty deep this year. We're working on a yearbook, and to describe school and his teacher, he made short work of it. School – I hate it. Teacher – Fat! Very honest, nothing hidden, but it sure was no praise to me. Oh well, I know he likes me, he just doesn't know how else to describe me.

I had visitors all day on Friday. Among them were Aunt Eva Beiler and her buddies. I didn't know them, but after sharing our lunch together, they felt like old friends. Even if I didn't get the schoolhouse cleaned, the visit was such a great spirit lifter. Thank you, girls! Ladies? Women?

[MAY 5, 1997]

Shrub-Trimming Controversy

Oh, I must tell you. I drastically trimmed two shrubs, in total disobedience to my beloved husband.

It isn't funny. Around this time each year we have our annual Shrub-Trimming Controversy. Gid thinks shrubs and trees look okay growing naturally. Every year I'd like to trim them, just enough so they don't look sloppy. He won't let me touch them. So Friday evening when he came home, he sat on the trampoline to talk while I trimmed, and we really liked each other. So I thought, "He really likes me. I'll trim the two worst ones." They are growing into the azaleas and all over the sidewalk. So while he took a nap, I got the wheelbarrow and whacked them way back. Halfway through, here he comes. Whoops. He just smiled and said it looks ugly. That's ALL! Now, I have plans for two more, then I won't push my luck any further.

I think doing only four shrubs still comes under the submission category, don't you, Eva Beiler and friends? SMILE.

[MAY 5, 1997]

A Gorgeous Day

What a gorgeous day! There's no other way to describe it except just plain gorgeous! Azaleas are in full bloom, clematis vines are ready to burst their buds, petunias are shyly opening their colors, and the grass is a lush green. One thing about our cool, dry spring, it made short work of the dandelions.

[MAY 12, 1997]

Absence Makes the Heart Grow Fonder

On Thursday, Joe Blanks had a buddy gathering. There were around 150 people, and we all brought a hot and cold dish. Gid and I enjoyed it very much.

Yep, Gid went along, and in the afternoon he wanted me to go to town with him. That evening David Bylers paid us a visit, and David thought maybe we should take Gid's temperature to see if he's all right. Then he went to the school sale all day. I was almost in shock! But, oh, it was so wonderful. Now, everyone says, absence makes the heart grow fonder, and it sure seems to work that way. It's not really our choice that he goes on "stay-aways"—but sometimes we have to do what we know is a necessity.

[MAY 12, 1997]

Dad Kauffman

Dad Kauffman is not very well lately. His throat and nose dry out, making his breathing so difficult at night. Mom gets so little sleep, being up at all hours with him, that she is fighting a sore throat all spring. Dad is also tormented with a yeast infection behind his ears and under his arms. They have tried just about anything, both medical and natural, and nothing seems to help.

We had company from Troutville at school, and one lady said sugar is the worst thing. Also all white flours. So now, Mom is trying to control his diet, which is no easy task, as he loves his food.

Israels took Dads to Juniata on Thursday. They spent some time at the river, then visited Uncle Abe Weavers. Dad was so tired out on the way home that Mom said they'll just have to eliminate their traveling, much as Dad enjoys it. So they need our prayers, those of the community, and friends near and far. Mail is something Dad really looks forward to.

[MAY 12, 1997]

Happy Mother's Day

Amos Fisher (or Stoltzfus?) who has Country Cards in Perry County had his stand set up at the school sale. The little girls had a small brown bag on the way home, held a bit secretively. Later that evening I noticed how quiet everything was, except an occasional rustle and giggle upstairs. Soon they crept up behind my recliner and deposited three homemade Mother's Day cards, candy, bookmarkers, a small plant in a clay pot, and erasers. They were all bursting with pride as I exclaimed over each item. I really detest sour candy and quite innocently stuck a purple "whateveritwas" into my mouth. Sheer force of will kept that thing in there, so as not to hurt their feelings...whew!

[MAY 12, 1997]

School's Out

School is over. I had been looking forward to it for quite some time, but still, on the last day, when the children sang our favorite songs, a huge lump formed in my throat. I'll just substitute a lot for Laura. These past two years have been a good experience, but I am looking forward to a more peaceful lifestyle.

. . . . .

It couldn't possibly be more peaceful than at this moment. Everyone is still sound asleep. Kendall is asleep on the couch, the clock ticking away. Mom Byler has sister's day today, and Rhoda has buddies' day, so there will be plenty of activity around here.

[MAY 20, 1997]

When I Was a Child...

On Sunday, Dad Bylers visited us awhile. We got a new wagon, a huge one with rubber tires, from Elmers. Mom Byler was worrying how fast the children are going, and Dad said he used to take lots of wagon rides when he was a child, and there's nothing so dangerous about it. So Gid challenged him to a ride. No problem. Dad went off a flying, down around the barn, while everyone stood on top of the hill, slapping their knees and laughing. He disappeared and didn't come back for quite some time. Yes, he did tip over, but wasn't seriously hurt, and laughed along with the rest of us.

[MAY 20, 1997]

Those Shrubs

The shrub argument opened again this weekend. Gid is building an old people's home in Philadelphia, in an affluent neighborhood, and he claimed those wealthy people don't trim their shrubs. They don't even have much of a yard, just shrubs growing naturally, and those shrubs I clipped are going to die.

I thought, "Good, I hope they do." But I said, "I'm sure they have landscapers and the whole works who trim them to look natural." He insisted they are natural. So I replied huffily, "Who cares? We're not wealthy people living in a Philadelphia suburb, and I don't like shrubs growing all over the sidewalk." So now I pushed my luck too far, and am just thinking of tying some earthly possessions in a red handkerchief on a stick, and walking down the road muttering to myself about submission, shrubs, husbands, and this cruel world.

From henceforth, I will not touch the shrubs, and if our visitors have to step over them to get to the door, and part shrubs to knock on the door, I'll be inside singing cheerily, with a lamp lit, 'cause the shrubs obscure all the sunlight. But I'll be singing, 'cause I finally learned to submit to my dear husband.

[MAY 20, 1997]

No Crying Today

This morning I set Emily on the bathroom counter to comb her hair. She seriously shook her finger at me, and solemnly announced, "Now Mom, I don't want you to do anything mean to me today." I asked why not, and she told me Anna will give her a prize if she doesn't cry today. Well, good for Anna. Emily has such an iron will, and if she's not allowed a certain doll or toy, she howls and just has one of her deep depressions. The other girls get so tired of it, and I have patience for a certain length of time till I turn to the age-old threat, "Now if you don't quit your fighting, I'm gonna get my paddle." So wise little Anna thought of an alternative, even if it's a dubious one.

[JUNE 2, 1997]

Pets and More Pets

Ben Byler had a frolic for the relatives to help on his new shop. They have a black Lab with a litter of puppies, and Andy wants one—not just Andy, Gid and the girls, too.

I just held my peace and listened. Otis is bored when Andy goes to work. We'd name the new dog Oscar, for Otis and Oscar. He wouldn't dig flower beds or chew stuff or anything, because Otis doesn't. Otis would teach him by being a good example.

When they finished, I said, "No, we have a nice, well-behaved dog. No. That's it." No one took me seriously. They're still talking about little Oscar. Well, that's fine. I have no intentions of giving in.

There are rabbits all over the place. The cat population is thriving. The air is full of pheasant, bantam, and rooster calls. The peacock screeches any old time of night or day, and the last thing we need is an Oscar.

The little girls' rabbits are named Precious Jewel, Peter, and Pearl. They play with them for hours, wrapped in blankets. Anna went with Joe Blanks to Carlisle Auction and came home with another rabbit. They named him Pickle. I hope Pickle never needs to know his own name. Poor bunny.

[JUNE 2, 1997]

Silly Writings

We all read and enjoyed a letter from some friends, and shared it with family on both sides. How true that is. We go through life and don't realize the seriousness of our fragile existence. I felt extremely silly writing about our arguments, etc.

When I write these things, I am never truly serious. As any married couple knows, we all have our times, some more so than others. And we're outspoken with all our thoughts and feelings, and discuss things loud and long, where others might be more reserved. Gid and I have never pretended to have a perfect marriage, since we're both very imperfect.

I caught him reading the "shrub" letter, and a slow grin spread across his face.

[JUNE 9, 1997]

Just Stay Calm, Mom

So, it was church Sunday as usual. Dinner, supper, and singing for the youth in the evening. We had a well-attended, respectful singing, and thank you to all the ones who attended. I love to hear a table full of singing boys and girls.

Getting ready for church around here seems very simple with two girls to help. But I am convinced that one girl is more than two. Friday morning is usually when the pressure's on, and I tackled the laundry while the girls started cleaning upstairs. Supposedly. I came back to the kitchen a while later, to find them all around the table, cereal and bagels everywhere, fussing, talking, and singing all at once.

It must have been a fright, as the clock was even crooked on the wall. Becky got up with a "Now, calm down, Mom. Just stay calm. We'll go now. We were just talking." Suppressed steam gave me a headache the rest of the day. Usually when Laura goes to work, Becky "kicks in" and things get done.

[JUNE 9, 1997]

This Wagon

This wagon. The girls walked to the greenhouse for mulch, as Becky's cottage needed sprucing up for church.

The door burst open a while later, and Anna was the picture of indignation. Sweating, her face red, and glasses slipping down her nose, she yelled, "I am never going for another wagon ride with Becky as long as I live." Her life span only reached to the next wagon ride, I suppose.

Another red face, Rosanne's, followed, and holding up two fingers she said, "We tipped this close."

Becky described the ride, trying to be serious. They can coast downhill for a long way, but must maneuver that huge wagon around turns, on a gravel road. They all sat perched on bags of mulch, with Becky driving, of course. She couldn't reach the brakes properly, so she just let it roll. It must have been quite a wild experience, and Laura and I tried to be sympathetic, but were soon laughing till we almost cried.

To imagine Becky leaning intently on the handle, with two terrified girls, on two wheels, who could keep a straight face?

[JUNE 9, 1997]

Going Home for Food

On Tuesday Eva and I spent the day at Dads. We quilted for Mom, and mostly sat around and ate. Mom always has a coffee break that spreads over the whole table, and when we're finished with break, it's time to start dinner.

She just has a way with food—fresh fruit, vegetables and dip, etc., and homemade vegetable and tuna noodle soup with huge sandwiches for lunch. Is it any wonder we love to go home?

I doubt very much if my girls will return home for the food. I had another miserable failure at baking last week again. What a flop! I found a recipe for Mississippi Mud Bars in a magazine, and since it was a combination of coconut and chocolate, I thought, "Yum." This time, my brave determination will carry me through. Well, they were truly inedible, the icing was too dark and runny, and it made the coconut and nuts look like strange objects. The only person to eat them was Laura, and she only did it to be kind, bless her heart. I know how gross they were.

[JUNE 16, 1997]

Better Than Insurance

Israel's Joseph had minor surgery to repair a tear in the retina of his eye. The doctor felt it was best to repair it now, rather than have trouble with it in later years. It was done in his office, but Joseph endured quite a bit of pain the remainder of the day.

Upon learning they had no insurance, the doctor said if they throw in an apple pie, he would see what he could do. Eva took a big apple pie, and his fee was cut exactly in half! Maybe that's our answer to the cost of hospitals. Apple pie.

[JUNE 16, 1997]

Too Young for an Overnighter

When little Kendall's mom came for her on Friday evening, she cried, 'cause she didn't want to go home. So she stayed till 9:00, and she still wasn't ready to go. We told her to stay for the night. All was well till 10:30, time to settle down, and she really got the blues. "I want my Mee-Maw!" So her grandmother came to get her, and we agreed a two-year-old is a bit small to stay for the night.

Emily has often begged to stay at Amos Blanks, so a while ago we let her. All was fine till Amos went up the stairs with the girls to say their prayers and tuck them in. Boy, did Emily get the blues! She thought she had to sleep with Amos, and Ruthie ended up having to rock her.

[JUNE 16, 1997]

From Your Secret Admirer

Strawberries are waiting, and Laura and Becky are getting absolutely nothing accomplished. Laura figured she can catch forty winks while I write, and Becky took off for greener pastures. No one likes to pick strawberries around here. Tomorrow we have peas to pick—what a moaning and groaning.

. . . . .

Becky received a letter in the mail, typewritten, from a "secret admirer." She is only thirteen, so this letter caused quite an uproar in our household. The first thing Becky did was call Mollie, and Mollie exclaimed and fussed accordingly.

On Friday Mollie spent the day here, and when Phil came to get her, they told Becky the letter was from Mollie! For once in her life, she was completely speechless.

[JUNE 16, 1997]

Rosie or Alma Lee

Dad Byler and Gid hitched up the colt to a cart and drove her on Saturday. She almost acted as if she knew what this is all about and trotted along as smoothly as any driving horse until she became tired.

Dad named her Rosie, and Andy named her Alma Lee, so I still don't know who she really is.

[JUNE 23, 1997]

Unprintable Argument

No news from the Byler household. No arguments, nothing really worth writing about. I'd think everyone would be thoroughly fed up with my *gafuss*, especially the people who don't really like me.

Gid, Andy, and I had a serious argument. I wouldn't write that in *Die Botschaft*. It was about Andy's peacock, which screeched day and night after his mate died. I honestly thought I couldn't take one more screech. He sounded like a tomcat, amplified many times, and this time, no joke at all, it wasn't funny. The peacock was turned loose, and I really hope he's in Africa by now.

[JUNE 23, 1997]

Best Chicken Ever

Laura is finished at the greenhouse, and life is settling into one long, lovely vacation. We're all so relaxed, and supper lasts for most of the evening, because Gid is at home.

They're working in Harrisburg, so I get up at 3:30 to pack his lunch, and Andy's at 5:30.

Last night we tried something new. I marinated chicken in Italian dressing, then Gid grilled it on the top rack, with cookie sheets to catch the drippings. It was the best we've ever tried. Yum. Gid loves to cook on the grill, and does a good job. Chicken along with fresh fruit and a salad makes a lovely supper. I'm on a diet.

Try Gid Fisher's dipping mustard.

[JUNE 23, 1997]

Peas and Knepp

On Thursday Laura and I helped *Mommy* Lydia Byler do her yard and flower beds. Laura planted flowers and mulched, while I mowed and raked. Sarah and Emma came over to help, and we sat under the plum tree, eating watermelon.

Grandma made "peas and *knepp*," which we had never eaten, along with canned sausage, rhubarb sauce, homemade bread with pear honey, and to top it all off, a Montgomery pie. It was all so old-fashioned and delicious. Laura and I just rolled our eyes at each other, meaning, "Oh, wow." *Knepp* are homemade dumplings, and Grandma doesn't measure, she just uses flour, egg, etc. I can just imagine my *knepp*. You'd probably have to cut them out with a router, and they could truly be used as real buttons.

[JUNE 30, 1997]

Becky Visits Mollie

Mollie spent the day here on Friday, and they hatched this really terrific idea of letting Becky go home with her. They've been close friends for six years, and Becky has never seen where Mollie lives. She was so excited. I talked to her on the phone, and she does not want to come home and talked as fast as she could describing everything in minute detail. Her descriptions start with, "Mom, you have never in your entire life seen so and so and so."

She attended a 4-H meeting about cows, went along to church, and today they want to visit every little shop in East Berlin. I just hope I can absorb everything I will hear when she returns, and stay alert and interested. She will describe everything she saw, felt, heard, and discovered. I told Gid I just can't imagine Laura and Becky being in the same family.

Laura is much more reserved and

level-headed, while Becky just explodes with energy. She's always with people, having something going, while Laura would rather curl up with a book. It's so interesting having a family, and as they grow, you learn to respect each child's personality. I would much rather have this time, than when they were all small, and you were so harassed and busy, with babies crying.

[JUNE 30, 1997]

A Growing Boy

Andy is growing so fast this summer. I can never put enough in his lunch. He just devours everything in sight. He's a good three inches taller than I am, and starting to pass Laura. He pulls himself up as tall as possible, but he still has a way to go to be taller than Gid.

[JUNE 30, 1997]

A Good, Old-Fashioned "Whop"

Kendall, the little girl we keep, does not want to go home anymore. She kicks and screams the whole way out the road. She wants to stay with "Emmy," and just loves to be here. It's interesting to watch her mother work with her, trying to persuade her to go along home. I bite my tongue, and sometimes I imagine I hear this faint hissing of steam coming out my ears. I would administer a few old-fashioned "whops" and that would be the end of the screaming, I'm afraid. We dearly love her, but I cannot imagine working for 30 minutes to persuade a two-year-old to go home. Maybe I'm wrong, but discipline is a very necessary part of loving a child.

[JUNE 30, 1997]

Dad Kauffman in ER

Dad Kauffman was taken to the ER during the night, with choking sensations in his throat, and being unable to breathe. Oxygen only worsened the situation, and the doctors took X-rays to make sure his lungs are clear. There is nothing they can do, as his muscles are so weak because of his MS. So Mom spent a stressful night, and the following day they sent for me, I suppose just for moral support, or someone to talk to. He drank a bit of juice, fell asleep, and felt better when he woke up. Remember them in your prayers, and send them a card if you have time.

Israels, Jrs., and we were all there on Sunday, and Mom made dinner for everyone. Ben Lantzes were there in the afternoon, and he was glad for the company.

[JULY 29, 1997]

Brand New Singer

I have a clothes basket piled high with a neighbor's overalls to patch. He said he bought his wife a new Singer sewing machine soon after they were married, and it's still brand new. I didn't tell him mine probably would be, too, if I was English! Although I do enjoy sewing, more than I ever have. The first week after school was over, when I sat down to sew, I always thought I had an iron heating on the stove. I think it was just leftover stress from sewing in the evening while I taught school!

[JULY 29, 1997]

Teacher Laura

Laura chose not to go to Perry County to the teachers' classes. I didn't say much, as she's much like her father, who wouldn't go either. And I, of course, would have loved it. But I don't feel as if she really needed it, as far as the first grade curriculum, or almost anything else. She had the same Mennonite teacher for eight years who used all these books. She went through all eight grades of School Aid English, and corrects me with pronunciation of words. But I have to help her with our old Strayer-Upton Arithmetic, which makes me feel smart. I think a good education is important, of course, but so is the interest and love of the children.

Becky is in eighth grade, and I'm hoping it will go well. Becky said she made up her mind that Laura is the teacher, not her sister, and she won't correct her, and will always listen. Good intentions, but…I kind of bow my head and hope she means it.

Laura and I went to Clay Bookstore and bought social studies books for 50 cents a piece. They have a good variety of used books, that I wished I would have had. Laura was never used to history and geography and thought the fifth and sixth grade were way too easy. We had so much fun, buying stickers, little erasers, and pencils for prizes.

We want to design her name charts, schedule, and rules soon. It's all so exciting as the time approaches.

[JULY 29, 1997]

Balloon Babies

The little girls have their purple tent set up on the front porch and are playing house. It's filled with blankets and pillows. Any ordinary mother would make them put it away, but I kind of pity them. They are having so much fun. Their favorite project this summer was filling balloons with water, painting their faces, giving them names like Rudy and Zeke, and wrapping them in blankets. These balloon babies only last for awhile, and soon burst all over their laps. Rosanne's had a pamper on, and when it burst she was left holding a water-laden pamper. Needless to say, they laugh and laugh every time it happens. I must run along and patch my neighbor's overalls.

[JULY 29, 1997]

Animal Lovers

Becky went to BB's Grocery to help Grandma Byler cut her cheese and lunch meat. She worked hard all day, loved every minute, and was rewarded with $20. The next day Joe Blanks went to Carlisle Auction, taking Becky along with her $20. Before she left, she said, "Mom, Dad said I can get a calf. Can I?" What was I supposed to say? Late that evening she returned with an $18 calf, a skinny little Holstein, with scours, as usual. SIGH. Well, she cleaned and scrubbed, fed and pampered the calf. I talked to Gid on the phone, and he said she has to keep it clean if it has scours. The calf has daily baths with soapy water, takes walks, and is brought into the yard.

Maryann said she was so nervous before she bid on this calf that her lap was full of fingernails and her knees were shaking. Now, whenever I need Becky to run an errand, she's nowhere to be found. She's down in the barn with the calf.

I don't understand this animal craze in my family. I never liked small animals or babies. Cats, bunnies, and all those small creatures always gave me the shivers. And when my friends always wanted to hold babies in church, I always made excuses. Why, babies clawed your face with their sticky little hands, pulled your covering strings, and most of the time spit up on you.

Of course, now I like babies, after having six of my own, but my sentiments remain the same about cats and bunnies.

[AUGUST 4, 1997]

Teachers' Class

It kind of bothers me how I wrote about Laura not needing to go to teachers' class. I certainly do not want to have people think we're smarter than anyone else. Certainly not. I guess to be perfectly honest, I found teachers' class a bit intimidating when I was a beginner. And as Laura lacks self-confidence, I hesitated to let her go. The teachers' classes are great in their place, but I feel the young teachers should also be reminded to use their emotions, inspirations, and methods of teaching. If we're not careful, we're too designated to have certain pages on certain days, and if we fall behind, we feel unfit and full of despair.

It shouldn't be that way. My first year of teaching I knew absolutely nothing about it. I just desperately wanted to teach. I had an old, old schoolhouse, half Mennonite and half Amish, and I taught by my own methods. There were no teachers' classes. I loved it. Then I could be spontaneous. If we wanted to try something totally new, we did! I'm sure we still can do that, but there is more "This is how you should do, to be a good teacher."

Although I remain a staunch supporter of anyone who wants to teach, should we not have a degree of freedom to teach in a way that fits us?

[AUGUST 4, 1997]

Surprise in Ohio

We just returned home from Ohio last night at 11:00. Mom, Eva, Ruthie, Betty, and I were out to Henry Hershbergers and Paul Millers, where Paul Betty planned a surprise for Vern's 80th birthday. It turned out absolutely perfect. All the cousins, and Mel Troyer Fannie, were all together in Paul's shop, and when we pulled in, Betty steered us excitedly in the right direction. Poor Vern. She was overwhelmed to begin with, and when Mom walked in she could do nothing but throw her hands in the air, and just holler with surprise. After every hug, she'd do it again, and was absolutely so taken aback that we pulled this off without her suspecting anything.

We had a delicious buffet lunch, with desserts that I just cannot begin to describe—date pudding, pecan pie, Jell-O, cake, ice cream, and coconut cream. Oh, it was unreal.

We spent a rare afternoon together, one we will never forget. It was truly so precious. Dear Vern, Fannie, and Mom, all sitting together, exchanging coverings, and looking at old school pictures. She received 80 packages, and is supposed to open one each day.

On the way home we were all so tired, and that last stretch of turnpike seemed so long.

Eva claimed when you go to Indiana the turnpike doesn't seem as long. I was half asleep, not adding to Ruthie and Eva's conversation, and suddenly I got this really deliciously funny thought, and burst out laughing. Of course, then I could hardly say it, but I managed to tell Eva I guess she must have had a head start, like a little car you pull back clear to Indiana, it went much faster.

So now this morning, feeling a little less than chirpy, I will return to my work. We have buddies' day here tomorrow, so we must bake and clean up. We wanted to do yard work, but it's raining, so we'll just have the buddies with an unkempt yard.

[AUGUST 13, 1997]

Bolts of Fabric

Mollie Van Lieu is with us again. I let Becky and Mollie go along to Ohio, and they really enjoyed it. They biked to Kidron and visited at the little shops, and just liked the idea of going so far away.

They went out to Anna Fisher's store and got bags of scrap material again. They cleaned out the little room where the girls had their doll house, and set up shop. First, they spent hours rolling the fabric on children's books, so they have bolts, and proceeded to price things. They played that for two days; now this morning I must get them to clean it up.

[AUGUST 13, 1997]

Gid in the Hospital

Another Monday, another wash day. The children are off to school. Andy is at work. Kendall is here playing with Emily, and the big change: Gid is at home.

When he went to the ER the second time for his IV, the swelling and redness had spread down his leg and they admitted him, to be able to have IV every four hours. He was not very happy about being admitted, as he didn't feel it was very necessary. He complained to the doctor, till he told him he'd look good with one leg. That kind of took the wind out of his sails, and he meekly gave in, being wheeled into his room on a stretcher.

I was waiting for him, and he promptly started saying he's thirsty and hungry and this is really crazy, etc. I was giggling inside, 'cause I knew how he hated being in the hospital, and knew how he'd sputter and fume, but there was nothing he could do. When his supper was served, the fuming started all over again. No salt! Boiled squash! Yuck! But we found packets of salt, and I thought the food was just fine. He didn't.

Anyway, he spent two days there, and enjoyed his visitors. Ervin Zimmermans spent an afternoon with us, as did Bill Moons of Bedford County and Dale Henry. Israels, Jimmys, Amoses, and Ben Kurtzes visited one evening.

The doctor says it was a bug bite, either a tick or a mosquito, that carried the infection. But because of his high fever, I was simply not comfortable trying to heal the knee at home, as I know a fever represents a serious infection.

So I'm hoping we made the right decision, even if a hospital bill is involved. I'm just not that brave to try natural or home remedies with something like this, and I think we should appreciate the medical profession, as we never know when a serious situation can happen. Or when we will really need them.

We're both very thankful to have the knee healing well, and he's about back to normal.

[SEPTEMBER 8, 1997]

Who's the Teacher?

Well, Laura and I hit our first snag on our peaceful river of having her teach. I was so determined I would not be bossy, or interfering, but…as it turned out, I kept saying something all the time. "Laura, the boys are not allowed on top of the bottle gas tank." "Laura, you need to tell the children to put their lunch boxes on the shelf after they've finished eating outside." "Laura, you need to give Anna more arithmetic. She's bored, and I really pushed them last year." "My, you had a lot of recess today," after we got a new volleyball net. It was Laura this and Laura that, till she became very quiet and Becky said she's mad at me. Oh dear, now what did I do? So I approached her, and she burst out, "Mom, it's like I'm not even teaching! I'm substituting for you!" And I felt thoroughly ashamed, as I was so determined she would not feel like she was under my shadow.

So we had a long talk. I promised not to do that, and she realizes we all need to take advice. I meant well, but I always find it harder to deal with her lack of confidence. I can't really feel for her, and all my badgering, don't do this, don't do that, just made her lose her interest. I know kind of how it is—even with pupils. Praise someone, and they'll try so much harder, but if you run them down, they don't care much.

So, here I go again. We learn through our own

mistakes, and maybe by the time I'm 80, I'll be an ordinary good person. 'Course, by then, I can get away with about anything, as don't they just excuse people over 80?

[SEPTEMBER 8, 1997]

Back at the Helm

I spent three days in the classroom again this week. We surprised Laura by doing lots of fall art, and putting brightly colored leaves on the windows. The upper grades decorated the blackboard with a huge "Welcome Back," and the lower grades wrote her a letter to tell her what they did these three days. I just love to teach school, and after scrubbing the floor and washing the porch and rugs on Friday, I walked home feeling quite miserable that I wasn't the teacher.

But when I got home and there was a whole weekend's work to be done, then I was glad I was Mom. My second graders remembered so much of our work from last year, when I reminded them, and their little eyes shone when it "clicked." I sure would love to steer them all through eight grades, although I'm sure Laura is capable too.

[SEPTEMBER 29, 1997]

Doing Dishes

While Laura was away, Anna had to help Becky with the dishes. She's not a very dedicated "dish-doer," because usually it's Laura or Becky and me, as I love to do dishes. Anyway, Anna kept disappearing. Becky was becoming more and more furious, and finally went running out the door in search of Anna. Awhile later I heard her "siccing" the two geese on Anna. We have two very bossy, noisy geese, and we all really dislike them. But they served Becky's purpose, and Anna promptly made a beeline for the house.

[SEPTEMBER 29, 1997]

Applesauce

Our applesauce making after school took way too long. At one point Laura sat on the countertop with her feet in the sink. Becky sat in one of the rinse tubs. Emily sat in the other, and we were all talking at once! We were all together again, out in the wash house, supposedly putting apples through the strainer. We talked and talked, and every once in a while remembered to keep going with the strainer. I really cherish this time, and try to store all the moments safely away for memories. Who could possibly be more dear than your own children? Perfect they are not, and as a mother I often fail, but I think children are just the whole reason we learn to slowly understand the term "unconditional love." They need so much of our time, our understanding, and our attention.

[SEPTEMBER 29, 1997]

Invader!

School teaching must have exhausted me, because Thursday evening after being sound asleep, I heard the door open and a man's footsteps walking through the kitchen. I grabbed my housecoat, and with my heart thumping so loudly I was sure the "man" would hear it, I ventured forward in the dark with a timid, "Is someone here?" Imagine my relief to hear my own Gid say, "Didn't you hear the truck pull in?" I always hear the vehicle and know it's him, but I must have slept too soundly, and was not expecting him till Friday. I probably aged two years in that tense moment.

[SEPTEMBER 29, 1997]

A Good Sisterly Time

The girls are all out on the picnic table "stamping," and singing "There's Redemption there for me, there's redemption there for me," while the four-square ball is being steadily thumped against the brick chimney playing 7-Up. Music to my ears, and I enjoy every minute today as Laura is not often at home like this, on a weekend. These five girls are having so much fun, and I tried to join them, but soon became bored. I would rather draw than use stamps to create something. But I do think it's amazing how "bought" these cards actually look.

[OCTOBER 5, 1997]

Allergic to Hunting

Gid and Andy are resting today, after archery hunting yesterday. Andy hunted with bow and arrow for the first time, and could hardly talk fast enough when he got home. He shot and lost every arrow he had, missed three deer, and never had so much fun in his life. His first time, and he must learn to wait till the deer are closer and be more careful. Gid asked, "Did any hunter ever get an allergic reaction to the deer scents you use to camouflage your odor?" Andy used something on his shirt, and almost instantly became so itchy that he was miserable. Hives swelled his right arm and over his stomach, and he went to the spring and kept running cold water over it to ease the itching. Gid said he was beginning to think he'll have to get to a doctor, when they discovered that every time he put the shirt on, it became definitely worse. His arm is still sore, swollen, and he has some hives.

[OCTOBER 5, 1997]

Okay Fatty, Buckle Down

I'm so fat it isn't funny. I am serious. My weight has been a source of much consternation lately. How could ten pounds creep up on me in two years of teaching school? I scootered six miles every day, mind you, and I still gained weight. I'm slowly coming to the sickening realization that I'm obese, one of those people who endanger their health by simply eating too much. Then I get up in the morning and tell myself, "Okay, fatty, today is the day. You will not get much to eat, and drink 64 ounces of water, and exercise." I hate to drink water when I'm not thirsty, and I very seldom become thirsty. So I eat a weeny little bowl of Raisin Bran, with 2% milk, gag on a glass of water, and go to work. I do well, with a bowl of soup and a skinny sandwich with no mayonnaise, till the children come home from school, and I love soggy sandwiches. So I nibble and eat, and tell myself I hardly ate anything today yet. And continue nibbling till I go to bed, assuring myself it's okay to skip my two-mile walk. I'm tired and was housecleaning all day. I don't believe in diet pills, or anything that tells you you'll lose weight instantly or has a miracle cure. I just need to be honest and face up to the fact that I consume more calories than I think I do. So either I have to accept myself and just be happy (Don't people see a smile before anything else?) or seriously learn to deprive myself of one of life's pleasures, which is good food. Is there anyone out there who has lost 40 pounds, kept it off, and lived happily that way? Oh yes, Sarah Kurtz, I forgot. She did, and it pains my conscience every time I see her. (Smile.) I really like her though.

Didn't I say my column would become smaller? You can see my willpower is much the same as my writing. As I write, I tell myself it will all fit in one column.

[OCTOBER 5, 1997]

Awful Geese

But I must write about the geese yet. To start our diesel when we wash, we have to walk through Andy's chicken yard. Those two white geese own their domain, which is the whole yard. Becky and I are really scared of them, and complain loud and long to Gid. He just laughs and says they won't bite. The last time I went to start the diesel, they were after me, head down, wings outspread, and making an awful fuss. I ran, and scratched madly at the doorknob to the diesel shanty, forgetting which way it turns. Now he can't tell me those geese would not love to bite my leg as hard as they can. When Becky goes through, she waves a broom and yells the whole way, but then she decided it's easier on the nerves to go around the barn and through the shop. It's always something around here, and I certainly hope we have roast goose for Thanksgiving and Christmas.

[OCTOBER 5, 1997]

An Apron for a Barrel

I was sewing today for the upcoming wedding in Ohio this week. It's hard to make an apron for a barrel. I opened the belt three times before I finally got it right. I was nice and patient, though, and just acted so good about it, until the hem was put in. I was ready to press it and congratulate myself, then I discovered it was too long. I just stood there, unbelieving. What did I do to deserve this? Bernina or not, I hate to sew at times like this.

[OCTOBER 13, 1997]

Those Geese!

The geese. Woe is us with the geese. Gid decided we'll put them in the pasture, and they can't get through the fence, and all our troubles will be over. The little girls are terrified to step outside, and you need a broom or a rake to start the diesel or go to the phone.

When we got home from church, there they were, in the back yard again. Gid started running after them, and ran and ran around in circles, over the flower beds, through the garden, until he caught them. It was so funny, how persistent he was till he cornered them. Back to the pasture they went, and guess who ruled the back yard today? The geese. They chased Rosanne up to the patio. The poor little girl's legs were churning like a piston, her face as white as a sheet, with this huge goose right at her heels. So I told Andy in no uncertain terms, the geese must go. But he loves them. He holds them, and talks to them, stroking their (UGH) feathers.

What an odd family, and all our odd troubles. It seems if one problem is solved, meaning poor Mr. Peacock, the bachelor, we have another one.

Otis just sits there and watches the geese with a baleful expression, as he is trained not to chase any fowl. I know he hates them. He looks just like I feel.

[OCTOBER 13, 1997]

Pictionary

Israel's Anna taught us how to play Pictionary, except you must describe the word orally, not on paper. They were playing most of the way out, and it really is an exciting game. The girls started Saturday afternoon, when Laura introduced it to Becky. They had a great time. Becky ran all out of control, and got so mad if Laura couldn't guess. The game ended with Becky stalking off and Laura helplessly laughing. Anna and I did pretty good, although age has its advantage, and Anna found it a bit intimidating.

[OCTOBER 20, 1997]

Active Imagination

Emily found an old case where Laura kept her contacts. So she puts water in each little compartment, and every morning she dips her finger in this water, pulls down her lower eyelid and sticks her finger in her eye. Her contacts are in now, and she's ready for the day. She became so engrossed in her new life that she made a house on the recliner with a washcloth, her contacts, sunglasses, and Kleenexes. She made a bed beside the recliner, added two teddy bears, her purse with two dollars in case she needs to go to Wal-Mart. She plays all by herself, talking nonstop about the condition of her eyes. Her imagination is so keen that I doubt if she'll ever be bored.

[OCTOBER 20, 1997]

Wild Animals

There really isn't much to write about. Otis is being a good dog. The geese are penned firmly in their allotted yard. Gid is on stay-away after hunting in Bedford County on Friday and Saturday. The children are all at school, and I have Becky's dresses to lengthen and an apron to make for Emily.

. . . . .

Oh yes, I could write about the coyotes in Bedford County. Jimmy and Jr. were out very early in their tree stands when their hair was literally raised to hear the most eerie howl they have ever heard. Jimmy just figured Jr. fell out of his tree stand and was badly hurt, when the howling increased.

They both realized it was an animal, not knowing there were coyotes in the area. There was a pack of eight, with a big black leader. Gid and Andy heard them Saturday evening, and Ben Byler was within 25 yards of a bobcat. It must be pretty wild up there. I'll just stay home and be thankful I don't need to hear the coyotes. They give me the shivers. I had to think of the time Laura Ingalls heard her first wolf, and their house was only half finished with only a quilt over the door. Eeeep!

[OCTOBER 20, 1997]

Keeping the Home Fires Burning

The girls are off to school this morning, and since Kendall is not coming today, I let Emily go along. She loves to go to school, and has spent many more hours in the classroom than most five-year-olds. She was awake earlier than usual this morning, hopping up and down in anticipation.

. . . . .

Gid left for Baltimore where he'll be working for three weeks. That means he'll be home every evening now for a while. Then they'll go to Philadelphia and stay away most of the winter, while I keep the home fires burning.

[OCTOBER 27, 1997]

855 644 8900
Medical

Eif

Donté 315-350-1087
Towncenter